Sharing Jesus
Effectively

Sharing Jesus Effectively

by
Jerry Savelle

HARRISON HOUSE
Tulsa, Oklahoma

Unless otherwise indicated,
all Scripture quotations are taken from
the *King James Version* of the Bible.

7th Printing
Over 45,000 in Print

Sharing Jesus Effectively
ISBN 0-89274-251-8
Copyright © 1982 by Jerry Savelle
P. O. Box 2228
Fort Worth, Texas 76113

Published by Harrison House, Inc.
P. O. Box 35035
Tulsa, Oklahoma 74153

Contents

Introduction
1 Be Willing To Go   9
2 Realize Your Authority in Christ   71
3 Realize the Integrity of God's Word   83
4 Before You Go . . .   101
5 Sample Approach   117
6 Follow-Up   123

Introduction

What is *sharing Jesus effectively*? You may sometimes hear it referred to as soulwinning, or personal evangelism, or witnessing. I prefer to call it sharing Jesus. I added the word *effectively* because in the past a great deal of "witnessing" has been non-productive. There are many reasons for ineffective witnessing, possibly because of wrong information that was shared or because those involved did not know how to share the right information.

In this study I want to deal with how to share Jesus *effectively*. Our goal is results. That's what we are after.

I don't like to do anything without getting results. I have too much to do to waste my time on things that don't produce results. That's the way we should approach witnessing. Sharing Jesus is something that is very effective. If you will take the principles outlined in this study and apply them to your witnessing, you will have success with every person with whom you have the opportunity to share.

Now you may think, *Yes, but everyone may not accept Jesus immediately.* That doesn't make any difference. As long as you plant the seed, God's Word will not return void. (Is. 55:11.) You may do the planting, someone else the watering. But if you will do the planting, that makes you a winner because it is God Who gives the increase. Once the Word is sown, God will not allow it to return to Him void. That makes you a winner with every person with whom you share Jesus!

Whether you see a person receive Jesus while in your presence is not the determining factor in successful, effective witnessing. The important thing is that you share the Word with others and that you believe God will cause it to be confirmed with signs following. (Mark 16:20.)

Some of the principles I will share with you may seem elementary and overly simple, but I have learned never to assume that everyone who enters such a study knows what I am talking about. Before we begin to build, it is important to first lay a foundation, to set some guidelines, to reach a level of mutual agreement and understanding.

I have proven these principles in my own witnessing experience. I pray that you too will come to understand them thoroughly and will allow them to guide and assist you as you share the Good News of Jesus Christ with others.

1
Be Willing To Go

And as he (Jesus) sat upon the mount of Olives, the disciples came unto him privately, saying, Tell us, when shall these things be? and what shall be the sign of thy coming, and of the end of the world?

And Jesus answered and said unto them, Take heed that no man deceive you. For many shall come in my name, saying, I am Christ; and shall deceive many.

And ye shall hear of wars and rumours of wars: see that ye be not troubled: for all these things must come to pass, but the end is not yet.

For nation shall rise against nation, and kingdom against kingdom: and there shall be famines, and pestilences, and earthquakes, in divers places. All these are the beginning of sorrows.

Then shall they deliver you up to be afflicted, and shall kill you: and ye shall be hated of all nations for my name's sake. And then shall many be offended, and shall betray one another, and shall hate one another. And many false prophets shall rise, and shall deceive many.

And because iniquity shall abound, the love of many shall wax cold. But he that shall endure unto the end, the same shall be saved.

And this gospel of the kingdom shall be preached in all the world for a witness unto all nations; and then shall the end come.

Matthew 24:3-14

Why Should We Be Willing To Go?

The first thing I want to point out from Matthew, chapter 24, is that you and I are living in the last days. There is so much fulfillment of God's Word taking place right now that I believe we are in the final stages of human history. I believe we are approaching the ushering in of the Lord Jesus Christ.

The Church is in better shape now than she has ever been before, and she is getting better all the time. I would very definitely say that we are in the period of time Jesus was talking about here. We have heard of all these things—wars and rumors of wars, earthquakes, famines, shortages. If you will stop and listen to your newscaster for just a few moments (don't spend too much time there though!) and read a headline or two in the daily newspaper, you will see that these things are being fulfilled right now.

Notice what Jesus told us in verses 4 and 5: *Take heed that no man deceive you. For many shall come in my name, saying, I am Christ; and shall deceive many.* Now that should indicate to us **why** we should be willing to go—because Jesus said that Satan will see to it that in this time, in this hour, there will be many who will come saying, ''I am Christ,'' and will deceive many.

This tells me that in the day and age in which we live, people are vulnerable. Do you know why? They are looking for truth. Do you know why so many people today are vulnerable to receive anything that is supernatural? Because, for the most part, people have not dealt with the supernatural. They have never before realized that the supernatural was real, and they have had very little knowledge of it. When something comes along which is obviously supernatural, they want to know more about it; they get involved in it.

You and I realize that everything supernatural is not necessarily of God. You know as well as I that today there is more knowledge of witchcraft, astrology, and the occult than ever before. There are more people in modern society who are not afraid to stand up and openly declare themselves to be witches. In fact, many things that are common knowledge to the world right now used to be things that were done only in secret, things that nobody talked about. Witchcraft isn't new. It has been going on for centuries, but only just recently has it come to the surface. When people see things that are supernatural, their natural curiosity makes them want to know more about them. That makes people today very susceptible to Satan and his demons.

Notice Jesus said that many people would come in His name and that many would be deceived. You know as well as I that when Jesus says something, it comes to pass. He wasn't just saying there is a possibility of these things happening; He was saying that they most assuredly **will** take place. Many false Christs will arise in the last days, and many people will be deceived by them.

The reason it is so important that you and I be willing to go is because Satan's agents are willing to go. Isn't that true? Satan's agents are willing. Satan has his vessels just like God has His. Why shouldn't he? You see, everything Satan does is a counterfeit, a perverted copy, of what God does.

Before Satan committed sin—before iniquity was found in him—he was an angel of God. His name was Lucifer, and he was called "the anointed cherub." (Ezek. 28:14.) He was a chosen vessel of Almighty God. He had great wisdom, insight, and beauty. He knew how the corporate structure of heaven operated.

After iniquity was found in him, he led one third of the angels in revolt against God's throne and was cast out of heaven with all of his followers. Then he set up a counterfeit reign in a spiritual realm which is unseen by the natural eye. In this invisible spiritual realm he has established a kingdom, modeled after God's heavenly kingdom. He has set up a throne and regime with an angelic host in imitation of what God has. He is trying to operate like God, still trying to exalt himself above the Most High. There is only one difference: Satan's kingdom is evil.

Satan's agents are willing to go. A good indication of this is the very fact that there is more knowledge of sin than ever before, more knowledge of witchcraft and carnality, of pornography and drugs, of everything Satan has authored. **If Satan's agents are willing to go and represent him, how much more should God's vessels be willing to go? How much more should the Body of Christ be willing to go to represent Jesus of Nazareth?** Satan's agents are bringing death to the people of the world; God's ambassadors should be taking life to them. If Satan's crowd is willing to go, then we ought to be even more willing to go!

Why Many Believers Don't Go

I realize that many times the reason people have been hesitant about sharing Jesus with others is a lack of knowledge. People feel that they just don't know how to share Christ with others. But really there is no excuse for that. You have a Bible, don't you? A lack of knowledge is really no excuse for believers today, because we all have a copy of God's Word.

If you don't know where to look in God's Word to find out how to be an effective witness, I suggest that you go to the book of Acts. That is exactly what the entire book is about — sharing Jesus.

If you want to know how to share Jesus effectively, I suggest that you read about Peter, Paul, Philip, and Stephen. These men were effective witnesses. The Apostle Paul said it well: . . . *our sufficiency is of God; who also hath made us able ministers of the new testament* (2 Cor. 3:5,6).

You see, all that God is looking for is someone who is **willing to go.** When you make yourself available, you will find that it isn't as difficult as you thought.

Why I Went

In 1969 when I accepted Jesus as Lord of my life, the only thing I knew to do was share with others what God had done for me. I knew that God had called me to the ministry, so I just started preparing myself for it in my bedroom. For three months, I locked myself up with tapes and books by Kenneth Copeland, Kenneth Hagin, and E. W. Kenyon. They introduced me to the Word of God. Before that time, I hadn't known anything about it. Then the Spirit of God took what these men had introduced to me and expounded upon it. After about three months of intensive study of the Word — of listening to tapes over and over until I was saturated with the Word, until it was coming out every pore of my body — then I was ready to preach.

My only problem was that nobody wanted to hear what I had to say. I didn't have a congregation I could go to. I didn't have any seminars scheduled. I had no crusades to hold. It seemed as if no one even knew I was in the ministry.

But I decided, "This is too good to keep to myself. I've got to tell it to somebody." So I went to the streets. I thought, *Well, I don't have a congregation. I don't have a seminar or a crusade set up. Nobody's invited me to come preach, so I'll just go where the people are.* I decided to get out of that bedroom, get in my car, and drive to wherever I saw people gathered. I thought one of the best places to go would be where the people didn't have anything else to do except listen to me. So I started standing out in front of some bars and lounges, waiting for someone to come out.

Somebody once said, "I sure wouldn't start my witnessing with one of those kind." I found out that the "outcasts"—the alcoholics, drug addicts, and prostitutes—were easier to reach than some of the people who had been in church. Most of the people I came in contact with who had been to church at least once in their lives considered themselves to be "saved." They would say, "Oh, yes, I believe in God. I've been to church. In fact, I'm going again on

Easter." These people were very hard to minister to at first, but I later learned how to reach them as well.

I soon learned that the drug addict and the alcoholic were looking for some good news. These people are searching for something, and you and I have what they are looking for.

That first time, I went down to a bar and just stood outside, waiting. The first guy who came out was so drunk he just barely made it through the door. I thought to myself, *Dear Lord, how in the world am I going to reach him? He's so drunk! I don't know if he can even hear me.* But I just talked to him anyway. I had no better sense than to believe in the power of God's Word and to believe that people **wanted** to hear what I had to say because it was the Gospel. It wasn't just something I had come up with—it was **the Gospel, the Good News!**

So I took this guy who was drunk and started talking to him. It looked as though he didn't understand a word I was saying, but I just kept sharing the Word with him. When I asked him, "Is there any reason why you can't make Jesus the Lord of your life right now?" he answered, "No, there isn't."

I asked, "Would you like to do that?"

"Yes."

When I prayed with him, he stumbled along through the prayer. Then the Devil planted the thought in my head, *Do you suppose he really meant it?* I decided right then not to give in to that strategy, so I told the Devil, "I don't know the thought and intent of this man's heart, but God does. I'm not going to judge by whether he cried or had 'goose bumps.' I'm just going to stand on what the Word says. Romans 10:9 says, *That if thou shalt confess with thy mouth the Lord Jesus, and shalt believe in thine heart that God hath raised him from the dead, thou shalt be saved.* This man did that, and as far as I'm concerned, he's born again!"

Then I just said, "Father, this man has said that he believes. Your Word says that if he confesses with his mouth the Lord Jesus and believes in his heart that You raised Him from the dead, he will be saved."

I asked the man, "Do you believe that?"

He said, "I believe it."

"Then the Bible says you are saved. I don't care whether you cry, or smile, or have goose bumps. As far as I'm concerned, you're born again."

You know, when that man heard what I said and took hold of it, he sobered up instantly. It was just as though he hadn't been drinking at all.

After that experience, I kept on witnessing with everyone. You see, then I didn't have any reason to quit. I mean, this was so exciting—why quit? Why quit when it was working? Word got around that I was having success at it. I was just doing what the Word of God said to do: *Go ye into all the world* (Mark 16:15). Many times as Jesus ministered to the blind or the sick, He would tell them, *See thou tell no man* (Matt. 8:4). What happened? Everybody in town found out about it within an hour!

Well, people started hearing about my ministry. I wasn't going around telling it; I was just doing what I thought the Spirit of God was instructing me to do.

The next thing I knew, people were calling and asking me to pray for them. They wanted me to go to a hospital and pray for a sick relative or friend. They wanted me to minister to a drug-addicted son or daughter.

Before long, we were ministering to ex-drug addicts. They were coming into our home every Monday night and bringing their buddies to get delivered. This was back when the "hippie movement" was strong in our nation. There we were with a houseful of long-haired, barefooted, stinking kids. They were bringing all their dope into our home, and we were turning it over to the proper authorities. My wife Carolyn had an uncle who was a detective, so we gave it all to him to see that it was properly disposed of. These kids would get delivered and they would bring their buddies to experience the same new freedom which they had found. We discovered that making ourselves available caused people to want to hear what we had to say.

I have shared all of this to make a point. It wasn't the name I made for myself, nor even the great success I had in witnessing. The point is that **I was willing to go.**

Now let's see what happened because I was willing to go, as the Lord has commanded all of us to do.

When I Went

A short time after this, Kenneth Copeland came to Shreveport, Louisiana, where I was living, to conduct a meeting. He heard about the success that we were having in sharing Jesus on a one-to-one basis, so he called me in for a talk. He said, "Jerry, I have some friends in California who are doing the same thing you're doing with great success. I want you to go out there and learn how to minister to some really hard-core kids. The Spirit of God has instructed me to pay your expenses. I'll call the man and tell him you're coming. I want you to go and spend as much time as necessary. When you get ready to come home, call me. I want you to share with me what has happened."

I had a friend, an ex-addict we had led to the Lord, and I wanted him to go with me. Before he was delivered, he had been on drugs for over four years, so he knew something about that kind of life. I had never taken drugs, so I knew nothing about it. The Devil tried to tell me that I wouldn't be able to communicate with a drug addict because I didn't know anything about drugs. He made me think I wouldn't be able to reach them because I didn't look or talk or act like them and didn't speak their language. But that's a lie right out of hell! It's not your knowledge of drugs that wins people to the Lord; it's your knowledge of the Word! It's the Word that reaches people for God, not our knowledge of the ways of this world.

But I didn't know that then, so I asked this young man to go with me. I especially wanted him to go along because we had been working together there on the streets of Shreveport. He had put me in contact with some of the biggest drug pushers in the city, because he had lived with them for over four years. We came to an agreement and God supplied the finances for both of us to go to California.

I thought there were some "strange people" in Louisiana, but when I got to Los Angeles, I encountered things I never knew existed in the world! You must realize that at that period of my life I had only been in the ministry about four months and hadn't been exposed to these things. Prior to that, I had been working in an automotive paint and body shop, protected from the world. I didn't know some of those things were even going on, like witchcraft and the occult. I found out very quickly that when you get into the ministry of reaching people who are involved in these things, you had better know your business!

We got out to Los Angeles around the Fourth of July. We joined a group of about one hundred ex-dopers who had gotten turned on to Jesus and went to a place called Pismo Beach. The young people had gathered there on the beach to celebrate the Fourth of July holiday, and we were sent to tell them about Jesus.

When we got out to the beach, we discovered that over a hundred thousand hippies were there that weekend. They were having one gigantic drug party with music, dancing, and dune buggy racing. This was in 1969 at the height of the hippie-oriented drug craze. You may recall what those days were like!

There I was, standing on a little mound of sand on the beach in California. As far as I could see in any direction, there was nothing but dune buggies, drugs, beer, and marijuana. I stood there with my little New Testament in my hand, thinking, *Dear God, what am I doing here?* I looked at myself, then looked at them, and thought, *They're not going to listen to me. I don't look like them or act like them. When I walk up to them, they're just going to laugh in my face!* You see, that's what the Devil was trying to tell me.

But, wait a minute, Jesus said in Matthew 24 that in the last days Satan's agents would be bold. Satan's

21

agents aren't at all ashamed to be ambassadors for him. There were thousands of them representing him right there in Pismo Beach! They weren't a bit timid about what they were doing! They were quite willing to do drugs and share them with other people. They didn't hesitate a bit to let you know where they stood. They were as bold as they could be!

As I stood there, I made up my mind. I said to myself, *I've come all the way from Shreveport, Louisiana. God paid my way out here. I'm not going to let the Devil beat me!*

I will never forget the first time I stepped off that little mound of sand and walked into a group of those kids. They were sitting in a circle, passing around a joint of marijuana. I walked into the middle of that circle and stood in front of them. I looked around at all of them and said, "Listen, I'd like to share something with you that has changed my whole life." Well, I had their attention. That doesn't imply anything religious. (The truth is, I didn't intend to share anything "religious" at all.) As far as they knew, I could have been one of them, introducing a new pill. After all, drugs will change your life.

Then I said, "His name is Jesus." That's when the snickering and the laughing started. My face got red, my heart started pounding, and my head started crying out, *Run, dummy, run!*

But I had made up my mind, *No! I've come this far. I'm an ambassador for Christ. Evidently God has confidence in me. He sent me here and paid my way, so I'm not going to fail Him! Praise God, I'm going to do my job!*

I was thinking all this, but I said, "No, listen, seriously, I want to share something with you that has changed my whole life." They kept on laughing and harassing me, but I just kept on talking about Jesus.

I didn't tell them they were going to hell for doing drugs. I didn't condemn them and tell them all the wrong things they were doing. That kind of negative approach, I found out later, was one reason so many of them were turned off to the Gospel. You see, we weren't the only group of ambassadors for Christ on the beach that weekend. Many churches had people out there witnessing and not all of them were doing it in a positive way. I remember one elderly lady, who was so sincere — but sincerely wrong. She walked up to one of those kids, handed him a tract, and asked him, "Do you know Jesus?" (I was standing close enough to hear the conversation. You see, I was learning to listen as well.)

The young man cursed and said, "No!"

The old lady yelled, "You're going to hell, you filthy hippie! You're going to hell!" Then she walked away, mad, kicking sand. The kid just stood there cursing her as she walked off.

Right then I thought, *This is a good opportunity to share some good news.* I walked up to the young fellow and said, "Hey, listen, I want to share something with you that has changed my whole life."

"What is it?" he said.

"Jesus."

"I don't want to hear it," he said. "One of your buddies just left here."

"No," I told him. "She meant well, but she didn't tell you the right thing. I want to share some Good News with you. You got a minute?"

"No, I haven't."

"Are you in a hurry?"

"Yes."

"Well, I'll walk along with you, if you don't mind."

He took off, so I just followed him. I kept sharing the ministry of reconciliation with him — not that he was going to hell or that God hated him because he was taking drugs, but the fact that God was in Christ, reconciling the world unto Himself, not counting men's sins against them. (2 Cor. 5:19.)

The only sin that separates a man from God is the sin of unbelief, not believing on Jesus Christ. All sin has been paid for. **The blood of Jesus has already solved the sin problem.** Jesus said the only sin that the Spirit of God would reprove the world of is the sin of unbelief, not believing on Jesus Christ. (John 16:8,9.)

I shared Jesus with him and he accepted it. Why? Because he had heard some Good News — the truth of the Gospel.

When I got into that crowd of kids, I realized that the reason they were harassing me was because the only thing they had heard about Jesus was the other side, the religious side. That wasn't what I was sent to tell them. I was an ambassador of Christ, not of the "First Church," not of the Baptist doctrine, or the Pentecostal doctrine, or any other denominational doctrine. First of all, I was an ambassador for Jesus Christ.

As I stood there, they kept harassing me. I remember one of the guys asked me if I wanted a joint. They did everything to get me to quit and run off. Well, that was an opportunity for me to find out whether 1 John 4:4 was true: Greater is He that is in me than he that is in the world.

Then I noticed one young girl sitting there with tears in her eyes, so I quit talking to everybody else and directed my attention to her. I sat down right in front of her and shared the Word with her. I knew the Spirit of God was ministering to her. It turned out that she was a minister's daughter who had been raised in a Christian home — a Full Gospel home. She had run away from home and had come to join the hippie movement.

God ministered to her heart. After I had shared the Word with her and led her in a prayer of forgiveness, she got up and added her witness to mine. She said, "This man is telling you the truth. I know better than this. I know Jesus, but I've allowed Satan to deceive me." Then she said, "I'm agreeing with him that the Gospel is Good News and Jesus is what we need." Right then there was a handful of those kids who came and wanted us to pray for them. As far as I was concerned, I had won the whole crowd because I had planted the seed in them!

There were a hundred of us out on the beach that day. We literally invaded the place. We made such an impact on the crowd that we heard about it several times later on through other people. Two days later we stopped for gas at a service station several miles from Pismo Beach. When the station attendant saw a Bible on the dash of the car, he asked us, "Did you hear what happened at Pismo Beach this week?"

"We sure did!"

"There was a group of Christians down there who led a whole bunch of hippies to the Lord!"

"They sure did!"

People had heard about it for miles around. During that weekend we baptized hundreds of kids in the Pacific Ocean. It was a real attention getter! Praise God!

The amazing thing was that when these kids got turned on to Jesus, they immediately wanted to go with us. You see, they hadn't been to seminary or Bible school to learn that they couldn't be witnesses. They hadn't been to church. They didn't know any better than to go and share with others what they had received. They wanted to go immediately! They didn't know God's Word, but they knew what had happened inside them, and they were willing to share it.

Let me share with you one of the highlights of the trip. I'll never forget it as long as I live. One night as we were out on the beach walking around, sharing Jesus with the people, there was a young girl with us whom we had led to the Lord earlier. She had been on drugs and God had miraculously delivered her. She said, "I've got a friend who has to hear this! Please come with me." We walked about half a mile down the beach, then we saw a guy coming toward us. It was almost unbelievable. He was crawling on his hands and knees, so stoned he didn't know where he was. He looked like a crab coming up out of the water.

This girl grabbed him and called him by name. He was the friend she was looking for! She said, "Look, I've got to share something with you. I've got to tell you what Jesus just did for me."

He had the wildest look in his eyes I've ever seen in my life. This guy was completely out of his mind!

His mind was blown, literally. He didn't know where he was, or possibly who he was! But she kept saying, "I've got to share Jesus with you. I've got to tell you what happened to me."

We managed to stand him up, but he just kept staring at us, wild-eyed. We continued to share Jesus with him, then we prayed in the Spirit. We were all standing around him, praying in the Spirit. Slowly, he began to sober up. Finally he reached the point where he could understand what we were saying to him. He accepted Jesus as the Lord of his life. He walked up off the beach and went into the little room we were using to pray with these people. Later we saw him on the street. He didn't even look like the same guy! He was completely sober, delivered, praising God, and wanting to share Jesus with somebody.

About that time another guy rode up on a motorcycle and stopped at a red light there at the intersection. This fellow on the motorcycle was rough looking. He looked like he could eat you alive! The young man who had just been saved and delivered from drugs said, "There's the one I want to talk to!"

I said, "Wait a minute, man! He's on a motorcycle!"

"I don't care," he said, "I know him, and I want to talk to him." He broke loose from us, ran out into the middle of the street, got right in front of that motorcycle, and straddled the front wheel.

The guy on the cycle was wearing a leather jacket with a skull and crossbones on it; hair was all over his face and hanging down to his shoulders. You couldn't tell if you were looking at his front or his back! He was drinking beer and waiting for the light to change. There was a wild-looking girl with him. She looked like she could easily have floored me! No doubt about it, they were a mean pair of folks!

My friend who had straddled the wheel grabbed the guy's beer, flung it away, and said, "You don't need that beer. You need what I've got." (I thought, *Dear God, what's going to happen now?*)

The guy on the cycle said, "If you don't move, you're going to get what I've got!"

But my friend went right on talking. "Man, I want to tell you about Jesus."

The fellow on the bike grabbed the handlebars and just jerked them around, throwing that guy off into the street. But he just got back up and straddled it again. "I want to tell you what's happened to me," he said. "You need Jesus."

He wouldn't give up. He just kept talking. "You know me. You know how my life has been. I came down to the beach stoned out of my mind. You know how long I've been on heroin, how long I've been on LSD. You know how long I've been on the hard stuff. Well, I've been instantly delivered, and you need what I've got. His name is Jesus."

Before long, that big wild-looking guy on the motorcycle started weeping. Tears were streaming down his cheeks. My friend led him to the Lord right there on the street. We later found out that he was a member of a tough motorcycle gang. For weeks that guy followed us around on that chopper. When he witnessed to you, brother, you didn't give him any lip! When he walked up to you and said, ''I've got something I want to share with you,'' you listened to what he had to say!

Another person saved during this time was a hired killer from Chicago who was on assignment in Los Angeles. I didn't even know there still were such things as hired killers. I thought that kind of thing went out with Al Capone. This man, a great big fellow, had been in prison for killing five men, and he was about to kill his sixth; but instead he received Jesus there on the beach.

The person who led him to the Lord was a young man, thirty-two years of age, who had grown up in an environment of drugs. This young man's parents had been on drugs before he was even born. He had been a main-line heroin addict for twenty-one years of his life. There wasn't a vein in his body that he hadn't put the needle in.

This young ex-drug addict led that hired killer to the Lord. I was there at Pismo Beach for twelve days, and that fellow stayed with us the whole time, leading people to the Lord. Then he went back to Chicago. I guess he went back there and began to lead others to the Lord, too.

Commissioned To Go

That experience taught me an important lesson: God will use anybody who will make himself (or herself) available. He will use anyone who is willing to do it.

It's not how long you've been born again that will make you an effective witness. It's not necessarily the tremendous insight you have into God's Word that will make you an effective witness. You can start with what you know now; and what you know now is what Jesus of Nazareth has done in your life.

Never get the idea that your testimony is no good because you weren't on drugs or because you hadn't made a horrible mess of your life before you met Jesus. I've heard people stand up and say, ''I don't have a very good testimony. I've known Jesus all my life.''

That's a tremendous testimony! There are people who want to hear it. So you can start now with what Jesus has done in your life. But don't stop there. You also need to get into God's Word. You need to know the Word that supports what Jesus did in your life. People are looking for evidence. They want evidence, and you can give it to them by the Word of God and by your own testimony. That's what a witness is: one who provides evidence.

As we have already seen in Matthew 24, Jesus said that in the day and time in which you and I live Satan's agents—Satan's vessels—would be going about deceiving many. If they are willing to go and represent Satan, then we ought to be willing to go and represent Jesus!

We also need to realize that we outnumber them! Praise God! There are more of us than there are of them. The more of us who go out and win others to Jesus, the smaller Satan's kingdom becomes and the quicker his population decreases. When we become willing to take the Gospel to them, then that enables them to be delivered from the power of darkness and translated into the Kingdom of God's dear Son. The more active Christians become in witnessing, the faster we will see Satan's kingdom begin to diminish. **But first we must be willing to go.**

In Matthew 28:18-20 we read a very familiar passage of Scripture: .

> *And Jesus came and spake unto them* (the disciples), *saying, All power is given unto me in heaven and in earth.*
>
> *Go ye therefore, and teach all nations, baptizing them in the name of the Father, and of the Son, and of the Holy Ghost:*

Teaching them to observe all things whatsoever I have commanded you: and, lo, I am with you alway, even unto the end of the world.

Many times people have the mistaken idea that this commission was just for the disciples. That's not so. The Great Commission is addressed to believers — **all** believers. You see, Jesus is actually saying the same thing here that He said in Mark 16:17,18. Mark translated His remarks this way:

And these signs shall follow them that believe; In my name shall they cast out devils; they shall speak with new tongues;

They shall take up serpents; and if they drink any deadly thing, it shall not hurt them; they shall lay hands on the sick, and they shall recover.

Mark is saying the same thing that Matthew said. The same commission is recorded in both places. The wording is just a little different. But you'll notice in Matthew 28 that, in the eyes of some people, it looks as though this is directed entirely to the disciples. It is not. How do we know this is not just for the disciples, but for all believers? Because in Mark's version Jesus said that these signs shall follow *them that believe.* Well, I'm one that believes, aren't you? Then the commission is for us, isn't it? It's for **all** those who believe on the Lord Jesus Christ—**all** believers. All of us are ambassadors for Christ, commissioned to carry the Good News to every creature.

Empowered To Go

Notice again Jesus' words: *All power is given unto me in heaven and in earth. Go ye therefore.* We could reverse the order and put it this way: "All power is given unto Me in heaven and in earth; therefore, you go." We would be saying the same thing.

In other words, this is what Jesus is telling us: "All power has been given unto Me both in heaven and in earth; therefore, since all power has been given to Me, you go into the earth, teach all nations, and preach the Gospel to every creature."

Jesus is telling us here that all power has been given to Him and that now He is giving it to us so we can go out and be witnesses for Him throughout the whole world. Of course, this power is to be used in our daily affairs, but notice that the main emphasis—the primary reason Jesus is telling us that all this power has been given to us—is to enable us to go into all the world.

Yes, this power is there for me to use to meet my daily needs and to overcome Satan in my personal affairs in this life, but you'll notice that the main emphasis is on our going. Jesus is telling us, "I'm giving you this power, this ability, this authority so that you may go!" Isn't that what He means here?

Now you might ask, "But what if I fail?" How could you? Jesus said, "Go, and behold, I am with you always." The Bible tells us, *If God be for us, who can be against us?* (Rom. 8:31). How could you fail if you go? The only failure we've been involved in is being unwilling to go.

If you go and share the Word, you will not fail, regardless of the response you receive, because God's Word will not return to Him void. He has said so. *So shall my word be that goeth forth out of my mouth: it shall not return unto me void* (Is. 55:11).

The only failure that we have experienced is our own failure to take God at His Word and do what He has told us to do.

While we are on this subject, let me say this: Mere willingness on our part is not enough. There are many people who say, "Oh, I'm willing to go, but . . . I don't know how," or "I'm willing to go, but . . . I've never been before." "I'm willing to go, *but* . . ." Whatever follows that "but" is one excuse or another for not going.

So we must qualify our statement about willingness. It's not enough just to be willing. We must be willing to go and to **perform.** In other words, we must be willing, and then do it. You see, the Bible says, *If ye be willing **and obedient,** ye shall eat the good of the land* (Is. 1:19). It is not enough just to be willing; we must **do** what we are willing to do.

Jesus has given us the power to go. He is with us, and if God be with us, who can be against us? There is no way we can fail, not if we are willing and obedient to do it. In Matthew 24:14 we read: *And this gospel of the kingdom shall be preached in all the world for a witness unto all nations; and then shall the end come.*

Notice the phrase *this gospel of the kingdom.* Christians are supposed to know this already, but just for the sake of building a solid foundation, so there can be no doubt about what we are talking about here, let's define the word *gospel. Gospel* is just another word for Good News. The Gospel of Jesus Christ is good news—not bad news, but **good** news.

Now it's not good news to tell the sinner that he's going to hell. He probably knows that already. He probably has a good idea now of what is in store for him. It is very likely that he has been told many times. He doesn't want to be told about hell; he wants to know how to escape it. That's what the Good News is all about. That's what the Gospel is: good news to the sinner about his situation. Don't you imagine most folks are interested in hearing some good news for a change? I think so; in fact, I *know* so!

Jesus said, *This gospel* (Good News) *of the kingdom shall be preached in all the world for a witness.* Now I want you to notice that Jesus said, *for a witness.* In the Greek text the word translated here as *witness* literally means "something evidential or with proof or with evidence." This Gospel of the Kingdom shall be preached in all the world *for a witness*—as something evidential, something with proof or with evidence.

Now with that definition in mind, let's read two other Scripture references and see what Jesus is telling us about going and sharing the Gospel with others:

And the gospel (the Good News) *must first be published among all nations* (Mark 13:10). In other words, "You must go and carry this Good News to the whole world."

And as ye go, preach, saying, The kingdom of heaven is at hand. Heal the sick, cleanse the lepers, raise the dead, cast out devils: freely ye have received, freely give (Matt. 10:7,8).

Somewhere down the line we have gotten the idea that witnessing or sharing Jesus meant just getting people saved, but the purpose of being a witness is to bring salvation, **full salvation**—spiritual, physical, and mental. Did you ever notice that was how the early disciples did it? They brought spiritual salvation, but they also brought physical salvation and mental salvation. According to Mark 16:20, *They went forth, and preached every where. . . .* They preached the Good News. And what did God do? *. . . the Lord working with them, and confirming the word with signs following.*

Many times we have been a little hesitant about sharing with others God's desire to deliver them from all their problems—not just spiritual problems, but physical, mental, emotional, and financial problems as well. The reason we have been hesitant to do this is because we have not always been confident that God would do it.

If you can build up enough confidence to believe that when you share the Gospel with a person, it will cause him or her to receive Jesus, be saved from sin, and be delivered from the power of darkness, then you can also build your confidence enough to believe that God will confirm your testimony about any of God's promised blessings. Why not go ahead and believe God will heal that person physically (or mentally, or financially) if he needs it? Why not believe that God will confirm His Word to free them from **all** bondage?

Many times healing becomes a "calling card" or an "attention getter." There have been times that before I could pray or share with some people, God first had to heal them so I could get their attention. As I have tried to share salvation with some people, I would realize that before they could be delivered from spiritual darkness, they needed physical attention. So I would share what God had to say in His Word about healing. When God had healed them, I had their full attention! They wanted to hear what else God had for them.

Let me give you an example. Once I was with Brother Copeland in a meeting in Memphis, Tennessee. When I was in the hotel parking lot, a drunk man walked up and asked me for some money. I took out a bill from my wallet; but when he reached out to get it, I grabbed his hand and wouldn't let go. I said, "I'm going to give you this money, but first I want to share something with you that has changed my whole life. I'm going to give you this, in the name of Jesus, but I want you to listen to me for a few minutes."

I told him, "You know, Jesus doesn't want you to live a life like this where you have to go around begging, never having enough to meet your needs. Your life is just being drained. Satan is stealing from you. Jesus doesn't want you to live that way. He wants to change your life."

I talked with him for about fifteen minutes, sharing the Gospel about how Jesus didn't want him to live like that. Then I said, "I want to ask you something. Is there any reason why you can't make Jesus the Lord of your life right now?"

He said, "No. I've heard about Jesus. I know about Him. I don't know why, but I've just never made Him the Lord of my life. But I don't know of any reason why I couldn't do it now."

"Well, then, I want to pray with you."

I grabbed his hand and led him in a prayer. As he prayed with me, the power of God hit that man so hard I could almost feel the impact of it.

When he had walked up to me, he was limping. I knew he was hurt physically, but I didn't say anything about it. Then the impact of receiving Jesus hit him so hard that he suddenly jumped up, unhooked his belt, and dropped his pants—right there on the street! Then he said excitedly, "Will Jesus heal this?"

The poor man had obviously been beaten up. There were bruises all over the lower part of his body. When he dropped his pants like that right in front of me there on the sidewalk, I was rather embarrassed for a minute. I said, "Man, what are you doing? Get your britches on!"

But, you see, the impact of receiving Jesus was such a reality inside him that he didn't know any better than to just ask, "Will God heal me too?" He didn't think about where he was. He didn't think about what he was doing. He only knew that he was hurting physically. He needed deliverance, and he wanted it right then and there! So God healed him. He walked off, and later showed up at our meeting.

I learned a lesson from that experience. I discovered that if I can believe God will save people, I can also believe He will heal them. He can deliver them just as easily as He can save them. There have been times when God has had to heal some people in order to get their attention long enough for me to deal with their spiritual needs.

Now I'm not telling you to go out into the streets and lay hands on everyone you come in contact with. What I am saying is: **Don't be afraid to.** Don't be afraid to minister to human needs, whatever they may be, in the name of Jesus. If you are convinced that God will save and deliver anyone who calls upon the name of Jesus, then you can also believe that God will meet **whatever** need that person may have.

This is what the Gospel of the Kingdom is all about. Jesus said He was anointed by the Spirit of God to preach the Good News, to heal the broken-hearted, to deliver the captives, to bring sight to the blind, and to set at liberty those who are bruised. (Luke 4:18.) Then He commissioned His disciples to go forth. He said, *As ye go, preach, saying, The kingdom of heaven is at hand. Heal the sick, cleanse the lepers, raise the dead, cast out devils: freely you have received, freely give* (Matt. 10:7,8).

A true ambassador of Jesus is not afraid to preach the Gospel of the Kingdom **in its entirety.** Jesus was telling us: ''Go into all the world and preach the **full Gospel.** I will be with you always to confirm My Word with signs following.''

Who Should Go?

Therefore if any man be in Christ, he is a new creature: old things are passed away; behold, all things are become new.

And all things are of God, who hath reconciled us to himself by Jesus Christ, and hath given to us the ministry of reconciliation;

To wit, that God was in Christ, reconciling the world unto himself, not imputing their trespasses unto them; and hath committed unto us the word of reconciliation.

Now then we are ambassadors for Christ, as though God did beseech you by us: we pray you in Christ's stead, be ye reconciled to God.

2 Corinthians 5:17-20

We have found out that the Word says Satan's ambassadors are willing to go; therefore, God's ambassadors should be willing to go. Who are the ambassadors of Christ? Christ's ambassadors are all those who are new creatures, created in Christ Jesus.

God says He has given unto His ambassadors the ministry of reconciliation. In other words, every Christian—every new creature in Christ—is in the ministry. You may not be in one of the five-fold offices of the ministry (Eph. 4:8-11); but as a representative of Jesus, an ambassador for Christ, you are in the ministry of reconciliation.

What is the ministry of reconciliation? What does it mean? It is defined in verse 19: *To wit* (or to know), *that God was in Christ, reconciling the world unto himself, not imputing their trespasses unto them; and hath committed unto us the word of reconciliation.* In *The Amplified Bible* this verse reads: "It was God (personally present) in Christ, reconciling and restoring the world to favor with Himself, not counting up and holding against [men] their trespasses [but cancelling them]; and committing to us the message of reconciliation—of the restoration to favor."

That's what reconciliation means. God was in Christ at Calvary; and through what Christ did at Calvary, God blotted out the sins of mankind. Now He is not holding the sins of the world against them. That's good news! Don't you think the world needs to know that? Don't you think they would **want** to know it?

The religious idea has been that the reason a sinner is going to hell is because of all the sins he has committed. But those sins have been forgiven. The reason a sinner goes to hell is because he does not believe in Jesus Christ.

All the sins you ever committed before you came to Jesus were already paid for by the shed blood of Jesus Christ at Calvary. The only sin keeping you out of fellowship with God was the sin of unbelief, of not believing on Jesus. All your past sins have been blotted out and canceled. They no longer exist! This is reconciliation.

The ministry of reconciliation which has been given to us is very simple: Tell others that *God is not counting men's sins against them;* they have been forgiven. When a sinner finds out that he has already been forgiven, he wants in!

But do you see the religious idea we have had in the past? We have told them: "You're going to hell because you drink! You're going to hell because you smoke! You're going to hell because you beat your wife!" I repeat: That's not what sends a person to hell! A person goes to hell because of the sin of unbelief. You must believe in God's Son and allow Him to be the Lord of your life.

A person goes to hell because he is not born again. An unregenerate spirit cannot enter the Kingdom of heaven. In reality, the ministry of reconciliation is simply giving people the good news that, through Jesus Christ, God has already forgiven them of all their sins and redeemed them to Himself—if they will only believe it.

I guarantee that if half the sinners in the world knew right now that they were already forgiven, you couldn't keep them out of the Kingdom of God! Do you know why? Because for years and years they have been beaten down and condemned. They have the idea that God is some kind of monster with a spiritual hammer in His hand just waiting to "bust their head" every time they do something wrong. That's the image of God that has been presented to the sinner by the religious world. But the Bible says the word of reconciliation is this: that God is not counting men's sins against them anymore.

When I witness to sinners, I don't condemn them. I don't even mention drinking, or smoking, or adultery, or whatever sin a person may be involved in. I talk about what God did for him in Christ at Calvary. I emphasize the fact that he is already forgiven of all his sins, whatever they may be. I present God's forgiveness and salvation to him, then I ask, "Now do you want new life?" Most of the time people will say, "I sure do!" Most of the time they will accept God's love and forgiveness. Sinners want to hear some good news!

You might ask, "But, what if they turn you down?" So what? At least you have planted some good news inside them. And, remember, you're not the only laborer out there. You plant the seed, and God will find somebody else who will water it. (1 Cor. 3:6,7.)

Every person I share Jesus with gets born again. Not one of them goes to hell, not one of them. Do you know why? Because I believe God will not let His Word return unto Him void.

That's how I brought one of my cousins to the Lord. I walked into his house one day and told him what God had done for me. I shared the Word with him—the ministry of reconciliation. He was on drugs at the time and thought I was crazy. He didn't want to hear what I had to say; in fact, he politely asked me to leave. I walked to my car, turned and pointed my finger at him, and said, "I may be a nut, but I tell you one thing, you're going to be just like me."

"But I don't want to be like you."

I said, "It's too late. I've already shared the Word with you. You'll be just like me. You'll keep thinking about what I've said until you have to make Jesus the Lord of your life."

Later he came to Jesus and was filled with the Holy Spirit.

I tell you, friend, *every* person I share Jesus with gets born again. Why? Because God says His Word will not return to Him void. I'm a winner with every person.

Someone once asked me, "How can you be so sure?" Because of God's Word!

"But what if the person deliberately turns and walks away? It's very obvious he doesn't believe what you say. What then?"

It's too late. The seed has already been planted. He may not act on it right then, but someday he will. What we have to learn to do is just let the Word work.

I remember an incident that took place one night while I was witnessing in front of Texas Christian University in Fort Worth. There was a place right across from TCU called "The Library" where students went in the evenings. I would wait around outside the door until some of them came out.

When one young man walked out, I started sharing Jesus with him. He said, "Man, I don't want to hear what you've got to say. I'm enjoying what I'm doing." But I kept sharing the Word. Finally, he said, "Look, I just don't want to hear what you've got to say!"

"Just give me one minute and I'll leave you alone."

"Okay, I guess one minute wouldn't hurt."

I told him, "Listen, the Word says, *If thou shalt confess with thy mouth the Lord Jesus, and shalt believe in thine heart that God hath raised him from the dead, thou shalt be saved.*"

"So what?"

"I just wanted you to hear me say that."

"Why?"

"Because now the seed's planted. You don't want to pray with me right now, but let me ask you one question: When the time comes in your life that you need Jesus, do you know how to receive Him?"

"What do you mean, 'When the time comes'? I don't intend to ever need Him."

"But you *will* need Him. What I want to know is, do you know how to receive Him?"

"What do you mean, 'how to receive Him'?"

"Let me say it one more time: *If thou shalt confess with thy mouth the Lord Jesus, and shalt believe in thine heart that God hath raised him from the dead, thou shalt be saved.* That's the way you get born again. Do you know how when the time comes?"

"But the time won't come."

"But if it did, would you know what to do?"

"Well, I guess I would say what you just said."

"That's right." Then I said, "Thank you," and left.

By that time, I had learned something you may want to use in witnessing. I had learned to go back to the places I had visited before. The people who came there would start looking for me. They expected me to be there.

So the next night at the same time I went back to "The Library." Do you know what happened? That same guy walked up to me, only he didn't come out of "The Library," he came around the corner. He walked up and said, "My God, fellow, would you pray with me? I haven't slept a wink all night!"

You see, the Word had been planted in his heart, and it didn't return void. I'm a winner with everybody I talk to about Jesus. I don't care whether or not they pray with me right then. I'm not trying to see how many people I can chalk up who have prayed with me. The main thing I am interested in is planting seeds.

Many times as I have walked away from people who didn't pray with me, I would say, "Father, I just want You to know I appreciate Your honoring Your Word. It won't return void in that person's life. It will prosper in the thing whereto You have sent it and accomplish that which You please. Looking through the eye of faith, I see that person born again; and I just thank You for it, Father, in the name of Jesus."

God's Word will not return to Him void, and it's the Word that we need to share. If I don't say anything except "Jesus loves you," then the seed has been planted, and it will not return void! That's the ministry of reconciliation.

The main thing that has caused people to fail in sharing Jesus is that they have approached it with a negative attitude. I know of people who have gone out to witness saying, "They're not going to listen to us. They don't want to hear what we've got to say." And they get just what they have said! If you have that kind of attitude, then you are helping the Devil prepare your way for defeat.

I don't approach it that way. I expect every person I share with to be born again. Whether they do it right at that moment or ten years later isn't important. As far as I'm concerned, the Word will not return void. If you will approach this with a positive attitude, you can be a winner with everybody you talk with.

Sharing Jesus is so thrilling. If you have never witnessed and shared Jesus with others, you are in for a real treat. There is absolutely nothing that can compare to the thrill you get the first time you lead someone to the Lord.

When we began, my wife Carolyn was very timid about witnessing. She would say, "I love God, but I just can't walk up to a total stranger. I'm just uncomfortable doing that." Finally, she sat in on one of the first sessions I ever taught on sharing Jesus with others. It was in a church in Fort Worth.

After the session, we took a group of young people to a shopping center to witness, and Carolyn went along. When we started, there were about 25 of us. By the end of the week, we had about 80. We led that many people to the Lord in a week's time!

I remember seeing Carolyn standing in front of a supermarket at that shopping center with a young boy. His head was bowed as he prayed with her and accepted the Lord. After that, we couldn't keep her out of the shopping center! Praise the Lord!

Sharing Jesus is a thrilling and exciting thing. And it isn't hard, if you understand what you are to do. We are not called to judge or condemn others for their sins. We are just called, commissioned, and empowered to share with them the Good News of what God has already done for them in Christ Jesus.

Believe me, it is much easier to take the word of reconciliation to the lost than to try to prove to them that they are going to hell. The sinner is already forgiven in the sight of God. What we need to do is let him know about it. That's the reason we are ambassadors. We are representing Jesus, telling the Good News.

It is we, the believers, who are to share the Good News. If we don't do it, it won't get done.

Why Is It Necessary that We Go?

For whosoever shall call upon the name of the Lord shall be saved.

How then shall they call on him in whom they have not believed? and how shall they believe in him of whom they have not heard? and how shall they hear without a preacher?

And how shall they preach, except they be sent? as it is written, How beautiful are the feet of them that preach the gospel of peace, and bring glad tidings of good things!

But they have not all obeyed the gospel. For Esaias saith, Lord, who hath believed our report?

So then faith cometh by hearing, and hearing by the word of God.

Romans 10:13-17

Here the Apostle Paul is telling us why it is important that you and I go. The reason is simple: If we don't go, how can people believe? How can they believe if they've not heard? Faith comes by hearing, and hearing by the Word of God.

Somewhere we have gotten the mistaken idea that everybody in the United States has heard about Jesus. It would be natural to assume that they have, but some people—right here in our own country—have never heard of Jesus. It was very shocking to me when I first discovered this fact.

A number of years ago I had the opportunity to minister in the Los Angeles County Jail. There were several of us who went together. When we arrived, the security guards told us that we would be unable to make any kind of physical contact with the inmates. We were told that we would be in one room and the inmates would be in another room.

I remember that we prayed together and believed God that somehow we would be allowed in where the prisoners were to minister to them. I wanted so much to be able to lay hands on the ones who needed it.

When we arrived, we met the prison chaplain who opened the service for us and then introduced a man who sang and led a couple of choruses. Then the chaplain turned the service over to me. As I started to speak, the chaplain suddenly interrupted me and said, "Wait a minute. I don't know why I'm doing this, but let's go in there where they are." We walked in where the prisoners were, just as we had prayed.

When we got in that room, I immediately noticed a young man who was sitting near the back of the room. He had long, shaggy hair. My attention was drawn to him, and I found myself directing the entire service toward him. I just knew in my spirit that when I finished preaching, that young man would be born again. I just knew it!

At the end of the service I invited all those who wanted to receive Jesus and be born again to come to the front. About 25 came forward. The very first one to get out of his seat was this young blond-haired boy. I walked over to him first, and I never will forget his words to me. He said, "I've never heard the name of Jesus before in my life. This is the first time I've ever heard that name."

This boy had lived his whole life in the United States without ever hearing the name of Jesus. He said, "I don't know anything about Him or about what you told us just now. But I do know this, He sure feels good."

That shocked me! There was a person in the United States who didn't know anything about Jesus. Right here in our country there are lots of people who have heard all kinds of religious ideas, but there are still those who have never heard of Jesus Christ.

In the Scripture passage set out above, Paul wrote, . . . *how shall they believe in him of whom they have not heard?* How can people believe in Jesus if they have never heard of Him? There are people who have never heard anything about Jesus Christ. That's the reason they have never accepted Him. It's one thing never to have heard anything, but it's something else to have heard the wrong information. There are many other people who have heard wrong things about Jesus, and that's why they have never accepted Him.

There are two kinds of unbelief. One is caused by a lack of knowledge; the other is a result of an unwillingness to believe. One person does not believe simply because he doesn't know anything that would cause him to believe. Because of a lack of knowledge concerning that particular subject, he can't believe. Another person has heard the truth but, as an act of his own free will, has decided not to believe. There are many people right here in the United States who have decided not to believe in Jesus because of all the wrong things they have heard about Him.

Once again as the Apostle Paul tells us, "How shall they believe except they first hear?" Why must they hear? Because faith comes by hearing, and hearing by the Word of God. This is why it is so essential that we become willing to go. If someone had not been willing to minister to you, you would not have heard the Gospel. If you had not heard, you could not have believed.

To hear it, you may have gone to a church, or to a Full Gospel Business Men's meeting, or to some other kind of gathering. You may have been told about Jesus by your parents, by some other relative, or by a friend. Maybe someone approached you on the street. Regardless of how it happened, you had to hear the Good News before you could believe it. If somebody had not been willing to speak the Gospel so you could hear it, you would not have believed.

Maybe you just picked up a Bible one day, started reading it, and came to the Lord on your own. Maybe you think that nobody else was involved in your decision, that it was just between you and the Lord. But that is impossible because the writers of the Bible were obedient. You were hearing what they had to say about Jesus through the written Word.

No matter how it came to you, you had to hear the Gospel before you could believe it. **This is the reason it is essential that we be willing to go. People cannot believe until they have heard something to**

believe. Our purpose as ambassadors is to make sure that we take them the right information.

I don't want to project an improper image of Jesus. Do you? I don't want to present a distorted image of God. As I have already pointed out, many people have not believed on Jesus because of the distorted image of God they have received. (Many times that distorted image has come from Christians.) They see God as some kind of vicious tyrant who is just looking for an opportunity to ''bust them over the head'' the first time they do something wrong or get the least bit out of line. The idea that all I have to look forward to was His knocking me out every time I made a mistake would keep me from wanting to become one of His children, too.

God is a God of love, mercy, compassion, kindness, and goodness; but how can people know the truth if we don't go tell them?

God loves them so much that *he gave his only begotten Son, that whosoever believeth in him should not perish, but have everlasting life* (John 3:16); but how will they know unless we tell them?

Jesus came *that they might have life, and that they might have it more abundantly* (John 10:10); but how will they know if we don't go tell them?

Why is it necessary that we go? Because if someone doesn't go, these people won't hear. If they don't hear, they can't believe. You and I **must** become willing to go. We are God's mouthpiece.

Where Should We Go?

To answer this question, we need to look at a parable Jesus taught His disciples and carefully examine certain aspects of it.

And when one of them that sat at meat with him heard these things, he said unto him, Blessed is he that shall eat bread in the kingdom of God.

Then said he (Jesus) unto him, A certain man made a great supper, and bade many: and sent his servant at supper time to say to them that were bidden, Come; for all things are now ready.

And they all with one consent began to make excuse. The first said unto him, I have bought a piece of ground, and I must needs go and see it: I pray thee have me excused.

And another said, I have bought five yoke of oxen, and I have to go prove them: I pray thee have me excused.

And another said, I have married a wife, and therefore I cannot come.

So that servant came, and shewed his lord these things. Then the master of the house being angry said to his servant, Go out quickly into the streets and lanes of the city, and bring in hither the poor, and the maimed, and the halt, and the blind.

And the servant said, Lord, it is done as thou hast commanded, and yet there is room.

And the Lord said unto the servant, Go out into the highways and hedges, and compel them to come in, that my house may be filled.

For I say unto you, That none of those men which were bidden shall taste of my supper.

Luke 14:15-24

We Have the Power

This parable has several meanings or lessons involved in it, but the first thing I want to direct your attention to is the excuses these men made for not coming to the supper.

Many times when God begins to call upon people to go out and share the Good News with others, most of them will come up with some kind of excuse for why they can't go. Please don't misunderstand me. I'm not saying that if you don't go out witnessing every night, God doesn't love you anymore. Once again, I want to make it clear that we are not to come under condemnation about this.

What I am trying to do is strike your attention. I want you to see very clearly that it is one thing to have the desire to go; it is another thing to go. Being willing and being obedient are two different things. I believe that we should set ourselves to determine that not only are we going to be **willing** to go, but we are also going to be **obedient** to do it. By doing that, you will find that all those excuses you had been making for not going become very flimsy.

"But, Brother Savelle, I'm not making excuses! I really am very bashful and timid. I just don't have a way with people. I'm telling the truth when I say I just don't have the ability to witness effectively!"

You may think you are being honest about your inability to share Jesus effectively; but really you're not being **honest,** you're being **deceived!** If you are a born-again, Spirit-filled believer, then you *do* have the ability to witness effectively.

When you receive the Holy Spirit, He enables you to be an effective witness. That's one of His jobs. It's the Devil who has been selling you the lie that you can't do it. Satan would love to come up with legitimate-sounding excuses why you can't witness. If you fall for these lies, you not only rob yourself of a tremendous blessing, you also rob the person who hasn't heard of his right to believe.

You *do* have within you the ability to be an effective witness for the Lord Jesus Christ. I can prove it to you from the Word of God. Let's look again at what Jesus told His disciples in Acts 1:8:

> *But ye shall receive power, after that the Holy Ghost is come upon you: and ye shall be witnesses unto me both in Jerusalem, and in all Judea, and in Samaria, and unto the uttermost part of the earth.*

Now I want us to do a little word study here. There are two or three words in this verse that I want to define from the Greek text. Then I will give you another rendering of this particular verse that is very powerful.

The first word we will look at is the word *power.* Jesus said, *Ye shall receive power.* In the original Greek text the word translated *power* is *dunamis.* It is the word from which we get our words *dynamite* (explosive power) and *dynamo* (self-energizing power). The Greek word *dunamis* means "power in action, as when put forth in performing miracles." It also means "ability, mighty works or miracle energy." A third definition would be "supernatural force."

When Jesus said, *Ye shall receive power, after that the Holy Ghost is come upon you,* He was actually saying, "When you receive the Holy Spirit, you will receive power in action, a mighty force, a supernatural energy!" That's the reason you can be an effective witness. Praise God!

The Devil failed to tell you this, didn't he? He told you that you couldn't do it. He said that you were too shy and timid. He neglected to tell you about the marvelous power you possess. Have you ever noticed how he avoids the truth? Well, I guess so! He knows what will happen if you get hold of it!

The Devil is telling you that you can't do it. But **Jesus is telling you that His primary purpose—His foremost reason—for filling you with the Holy Spirit is so that you may be an effective witness for Him.**

Do you remember what happened when you were first filled with the Holy Ghost? Did you notice how bold you immediately became? You may have become a little lazy since then, but you definitely recognized a difference between the day *after* you were filled with the Holy Spirit and the day *before.* After that experience, there was a new boldness inside you. You told people about the Lord that you wouldn't have dared to walk up to and witness to before. Why? Because when you receive power, you become an effective witness.

That is the first and foremost purpose of your being filled with the Holy Spirit. God didn't fill you with His Holy Spirit just so you could be called Pentecostal. God couldn't care less whether you become Pentecostal, or Baptist, or Methodist. God filled you with His Spirit so you could become an effective witness!

We Have the Proof

Now let's look at the word *witness.* Jesus said, *Ye shall be witnesses unto me.*

The Greek word translated here as *witness* is *martus*. It is the word from which we get our English word *martyr*. In fact, the same Greek word is translated *martyr* or *martyrs* in several other places in the Bible. For example, Paul used this Greek word in Acts 22:20 when he declared: *And when the blood of thy martyr (martus) Stephen was shed, I also was standing by, and consenting unto his death.* (See also Rev. 2:13; 17:6.)

Stephen was an effective witness; that's actually what Paul was calling him here. In the early Church when men first began to give witness of the resurrection of our Lord Jesus Christ, it wasn't very popular to be a Christian. In fact, so many people laid down their lives as a witness of their faith, it gradually became understood that a witness was one who bore witness by his death. That's how the word *martyr* received the meaning it has for us today.

Actually the word *martyr* or *witness* simply denotes one who can vouche for, guarantee, or prove what he has seen or heard or knows. That's what an effective witness is.

"So what has that got to do with us?" Just this: When we go out as an ambassador—a representative, a witness—for Jesus, we go as one who can guarantee, vouche for, or prove what we have seen, heard, or know.

If you are sharing with someone concerning the ministry of reconciliation, you first share with them what the Word has to say about it; then you are called upon to vouche for, or guarantee, or prove what you have seen, heard, or know about reconciliation. This is where your personal testimony comes in. It is your own personal experience with the Lord which proves God's Word and makes you effective in witnessing to others.

If you are sharing with a person that Jesus will give him peace and deliver him from oppression, then you ought to be able to guarantee it. And how do you guarantee it? By telling him what the Word says about it, and the Word says that God will confirm it. The guarantee is "Thus saith the Lord." You can be sure of one thing: If God said it, it is so.

God may have done that very thing for you. In that case, your own personal testimony would be a voucher or proof of what Jesus is capable of doing for anyone who will take God's Word for it. Your testimony of what God has done for you would back up what the Word says.

The Word says, *These signs shall follow them that believe . . . they shall lay hands on the sick, and they shall recover* (Mark 16:17,18). If a person needs healing in his body, then you shouldn't hesitate to lay hands on him, expecting God to honor His Word and heal him. As I have said, many times God has had to heal people first before I could get their attention to deal with their spiritual needs. Healing became the "attention getter."

This happened many times in the ministry of Jesus and in the ministries of those mentioned in the book of Acts. Miracles get people's attention. Many times when Peter, Philip, or another of the apostles preached, there were great signs, wonders, and miracles. The Bible says that many of the people wondered, and stood amazed. It also says that many of them believed the Word that was preached on those occasions.

The miracle is not designed to make a person believe, but to get his attention. Then what he needs is to hear the Word. The Word is what causes a person to believe, but many people want to see or feel something before they will believe. And, you know, God will "bend over backwards" where the sinner is concerned to get his attention.

Some people came into meetings like those held by Kathryn Kuhlman and, without believing in God, got healed of tuberculosis or ulcers or asthma or some incurable disease. How can people sometimes experience miracles in meetings like that and never believe anything? God worked a miracle to get their attention. God was helping the sinner by getting his attention.

So an effective witness is one who can vouche for, guarantee, or prove what he has seen or heard or knows.

We Have the Place

There is one other word in Acts 1:8 that I want us
to look at. It is the word *uttermost*. Jesus said:

> *But ye shall receive power, after that the
> Holy Ghost is come upon you: and ye shall be
> witnesses unto me both in Jerusalem, and in all
> Judea, and in Samaria, and unto the **uttermost**
> part of the earth.*

This word *uttermost* means "inner, hidden,
remote, last part or frontier." This word was used to
refer to what the Apostle Paul called "the regions
beyond."

So then, what was Jesus telling us here? He was
saying that He has filled us with the Spirit of God and
enabled us to have miracle-working ability, so that
we may be effective witnesses who can guarantee,
vouche for, or prove what we have seen, heard, and
know. He was saying that our witness will begin
where we are and should extend to the farthest
frontier. We can start right in our own neighborhood.
If the people next door have not yet been reached
with the Good News, then they literally become our
Jerusalem. Isn't that right?

Now I would like to put all these definitions
together and give you a powerful translation of Acts
1:8. It's rather lengthy, but it's so powerful I think
you will enjoy it. This rendering was not originated

by me, but was taken from a lesson on soulwinning taught by T. L. Osborn.

> *You shall receive virtue, miracle ability, supernatural energy, after that the Holy Ghost is come upon you, for a specific purpose: to enable you to give absolute evidence and miraculous proof of My resurrection.*

> *It is this power working in you that will actually demonstrate and exhibit the proof of your testimony so as to verify your claims as with documented credentials.*

> *And you are to exhibit this supernatural evidence of My resurrection in your own cities and country, and unto the inner and hidden parts of the earth—yes, even to the remote and last frontier of civilization.*

This is the reason you can be an effective witness. When the Holy Ghost is come upon you, you receive virtue, miracle ability, and supernatural energy which gives you the ability to demonstrate and exhibit the proof of the resurrection of Jesus Christ. Hallelujah!

Somebody has said, "Well, I don't have all that." Then get filled with the Holy Ghost and you will! Receive the Holy Spirit and you will have all this!

Now let me show you from the Word of God this miracle power for effective witnessing as evidenced in the life of the Apostle Paul. In the second chapter of 1 Corinthians, verses 1-4, Paul writes:

> *And I, brethren, when I came to you, came not with excellency of speech or of wisdom, declaring unto you the testimony of God.*
>
> *For I determined not to know any thing among you, save Jesus Christ, and him crucified.*
>
> *And I was with you in weakness, and in fear, and in much trembling.*
>
> *And my speech and my preaching was not with enticing words of man's wisdom, but in demonstration of the Spirit and of power.*

This is an example of exactly what Jesus said would happen when you *receive power, after that the Holy Ghost is come upon you.* The Apostle Paul says here that he did not come to these people with excellency of speech or enticing words, but in demonstration of the Spirit and of power. In other words, an effective witness is one who not only speaks words in representing Jesus Christ, but, if need be, can vouch for, guarantee, and prove his testimony with signs following. Simply stated, **an effective witness is one who can back up what he has to say with miraculous proof.**

But without the Holy Spirit inside you, you cannot do that. That's the reason people who have not received the Holy Spirit have found that they are not very effective witnesses. Oh, they can have results to a certain degree; but without the aid of the Holy Ghost, they are not fully equipped to deal with the needs of the people to whom they go.

There are some people out there who have some tremendous problems! I could share with you some stories from my own personal witnessing experiences that would "curl your hair."

Have you ever walked in on somebody who is just about to commit suicide? If you ever do, you had better have the Holy Spirit, or you'll probably be helpless.

Now I'm not trying to frighten you away from witnessing. That would defeat my very purpose in writing this book. I am just stressing the fact that there are some tremendous needs in this world. That's why you need the wisdom and power of the Holy Spirit. You might not know how to handle a particular situation, but the Holy Spirit would.

If we are going to reach people for the Lord in this day and age, we must be properly equipped to deal with whatever we may encounter. The equipment we need is the Word of God, the name of Jesus, and the presence and power of the Holy Ghost.

An effective witness is one who has received the Holy Ghost and thus has that miracle-working ability within him, that ability to vouche for, guarantee, and prove his testimony with signs following, if necessary.

Now don't misunderstand me. The witness is not the one who does the confirming. God does that. We are the ones who carry the Word to the world, just as the Apostle Paul carried it to the Corinthians.

Let's be assured on the basis of God's own Word that if we will go into the uttermost part of the world and share with every creature what God has done for them in Jesus Christ, then God will work with us and confirm His Word with signs following.

Why Should We Care about the Lost?

Proverbs 11:30 says: *He that winneth souls is wise.* This should be indication enough that God cares about the sinner and expects us to care also. If God cared enough for them to give His only begotten Son that they might not perish, but have everlasting life, then we surely ought to care enough to tell them about that love. Don't you agree?

Psalm 111:6 says: *He hath shewed his people the power of his works, that he may give them the heritage of the heathen.* Here God is telling us that He has empowered His people with His own miracle virtue to enable them to claim their inheritance of unregenerated souls. Did you know that the lost are the inheritance of the righteous? They are part of our inheritance, and the person who wins them is wise.

Why should we care enough about the lost to go? Because God cared enough about us to send His own Son for us. Now He is sending us for them. Do we dare refuse to go?

2

Realize Your Authority in Christ

I always like to add this to any study on sharing Jesus effectively. The reason is because you need to have a proper mental attitude before you go. If you are to be an effective witness, you must have a very positive attitude.

Don't go out thinking, "Oh, I just know this is going to be hard. This is a tough neighborhood; I just know these people aren't going to listen to me. They aren't interested in hearing what I have to say."

Don't approach it that way. That's negative thinking. To witness effectively you must have a proper attitude about what you are doing. The way to build a proper attitude is by relying on what the Word of God says about you. Don't look at the circumstances; don't lean to your own feelings. Look *only* at what God says.

When I go out to share Jesus, I don't allow myself to think negatively. The purpose of my going in the first place is to **win.** As I have said, if I open my mouth and share the Word with just one person, I am already a winner, regardless of whether that person gets born again while I'm talking to him. I've planted the seed, God will send somebody else to water it, and God will get the increase. I go out with a very positive attitude, and God honors it. I go out expecting results with every person.

You Have Not Received the Spirit of Fear

We need to realize our authority in Christ. We need to remember that fear is not of God; it is of the Devil.

Fear is one of the things that has robbed many believers and kept them from ever approaching anyone to share Christ with them. They have never been bold enough to say anything to others about Jesus because of fear: fear of what people will say, fear of failure, fear of being laughed at, fear of not doing it properly. Any excuse the Devil can use to cause fear in you is to his credit.

But the Bible says, *God hath not given us the spirit of fear; but of **power**, and of **love**, and of a **sound mind*** (2 Tim. 1:7). The literal Greek text says, ''God has not given us the spirit of a coward.'' I'm not a coward. I'm not afraid to share my witness, my testimony, and the word of reconciliation with any human being, regardless of his stature—whether he is of low estate or whether he is a king. God has not given me the spirit of fear.

I remember one incident that happened while I was flying from Los Angeles to Dallas. I boarded the airplane in Los Angeles, sat down, and got comfortable. I was sitting on the aisle. As soon as we had reached our cruising altitude, the flight attendant came by and took orders for drinks. The guy sitting across the aisle from me ordered a couple of mixed drinks. I ordered a soft drink, pulled out my New Testament, and began to read. In a few minutes this fellow ordered a couple more drinks. After the attendant brought them, the man mixed them the way he wanted them, then reached over and tapped me on the shoulder.

When I looked up, he asked me, "Do you go to the seminary?"

"No, sir, I don't."

"Well," he replied, "why are you reading that Bible?"

"Because I live by it."

"Aw," he said, and sat back.

I just kept reading. I could see that he was "ripe." He was interested, so I decided to just let him do the talking. I knew he would want to know more.

In a little while he tapped me on the shoulder again. "What do you mean, you live by it?"

"Well, when I accepted Jesus as the Lord of my life, I found out that the Bible says, *The just shall live by faith.* I live by faith; but without reading the Bible, I wouldn't know how to live that way. I live by the Word."

"Aw. I see."

I went back to my reading, and he remained quiet for a little while. Then he ordered another drink. By this time, he was getting a little high. We were flying at about 32,000 feet, so the altitude and the alcohol began to have their effect.

In a minute or so, he tapped me on the shoulder again. By then, he was beginning to talk a little funny. "Are you a preacher?"

"Yes, sir, I'm a minister of the Gospel. But that's not the reason I read the Bible. I read the Bible because I live by it. I found out that this is the only way to live successfully. I was a failure before I discovered the Word."

I had his attention then, so I just turned directly to him and started sharing the Word with him.

"Sir, evidently there's something lacking in your life."

"What makes you think so?" he asked.

"Well, I noticed that's the sixth drink you've ordered."

"Yes, it is."

"There's something lacking in your life, and you're trying to replace it with alcohol. Or you're trying to fill a void in your life with alcohol."

I let that sink in for a moment, then added, "There's just one problem though: There isn't enough alcohol in the world that can fill the void in your life where Jesus should be."

He said, "You're right." Then he broke down and started crying. Now the Devil would love to tell us, "You know how these drunks are, they'll cry at anything!" But it wasn't like that. He was sincerely touched.

We talked the rest of the way to Dallas, and I shared the Gospel with him. When I heard the captain announce that we were about to land, I knew I only had a few minutes to lead this man to the Lord. Finally I asked him, "Is there any reason why you can't make Jesus Christ the Lord of your life right now?"

He said, "No."

"Then I want to pray with you."

As we landed in Dallas, I had just reached the point where I was ready to pray with him. You know how everybody is always in a hurry to get off the plane when it lands. As we stood up, I grabbed his hand and said, "Sir, you're sure there's no reason why you can't make Jesus your Lord right now?"

"No reason at all."

"Then I want to pray with you. I want you to repeat this prayer with me."

Now the plane was on the ground and everybody was standing up to get off. As we stood there in the aisle together, I led him in a confession of the Word of God—not a confession of sins. If he had tried to confess his sins, we would have been there all day! To get born again, a sinner doesn't confess his sins; he confesses the lordship of Jesus Christ.

I led him in a very simple prayer, based on Romans 10:9. When I looked up at him, everybody around us had their heads bowed.

After we prayed, he grabbed me and hugged me. He said, "I'm sure glad I was sitting by you."

As we walked off the plane, he told me why he was drinking. He said, "My mother just died. I haven't seen her since I was a little boy because I ran away from home when I was very young. My relatives found out where I was and got word to me about her death. I've come back home for the funeral.

"I've hated my parents all my life, and my relatives have hated me because of it. This is the first contact I've had with them in years. I couldn't face them. I knew how they were going to treat me when I got here. Ever since I got on that plane, I've been condemned for not seeing my parents all the days that they were alive. Now they're dead and I'm going back to bury them. It was too much for me to bear."

By the time that man got off the airplane, he was a free man. Praise God, he was free!

Had I been afraid of what the people on that plane would think, especially when it came time to get off, that man would not be free.

The Devil would gladly have told me, "Now, wait a minute, it's time to get off. Everybody's in a hurry. Nobody's paid any attention to this conversation up to now. You don't want to hold all these folks up and call attention to yourself by standing up and praying for this guy right here in front of everybody! You would both be embarrassed. Everybody would be staring at you. They'd think you're some kind of religious fanatic or something."

But God has not given me the spirit of a coward. Regardless of the circumstances or the stature of the person with whom we are dealing, God has given us the power, and the love, and the sound mind to handle that situation—if we will just be bold enough to act on His Word. **God has not given us a spirit of fear.**

By the way, airplanes are a tremendous place in which to witness. It's unlikely that the person you are talking to can get up and leave. Where is he going to go?

Most of the time I don't start the conversation. I just sit there and mind my own business. Usually people will start talking to me. They want to know what I do for a living, or where I'm going, or even why I'm smiling! A good place to witness is anyplace where there are people!

I'm not afraid of people. I'm not afraid of what they might think or what they might say. I haven't received the spirit of a coward—and neither have **you.**

God Has Made You Bold

In Ephesians, Paul speaks of our position in Christ by saying, *in whom we have boldness* (Eph. 3:12).

Proverbs 28:1 tells us: *The righteous are bold as a lion.* We need to know that. When we become ambassadors and representatives of Jesus Christ, we need to know that we have not been given a spirit of fear, but that we are bold—as bold as a lion.

Many times when I teach these things in a meeting or a seminar, people will say to me, "But, Brother Savelle, I can't witness to others. I'm too afraid. I can't just walk up to a total stranger and share with him."

I always tell them, "What you need to do is start confessing the Word. Start confessing what the Word of God says about you. Every step you take toward that person, just say to yourself, *God has not given me the spirit of fear; but of power, and of love, and of a sound mind. I'm not a coward. I'm the righteousness of God, and the righteous are bold as a lion.* By the time you get to that person, you will be bold."

Someone will usually ask, "Yes, but what if it doesn't work?"

I always say, "Then start all over again!"

Just keep confessing the Word. You need to know your authority—who you are in Christ. You happen to be a child of God. You are not a loser; you're a winner! You're not a chump; you're a champ! God has not made you timid and fearful; He has made **you** as bold as a lion!

The Anointing of God Is upon You

In Luke 4:18 we read where Jesus stood up in the temple at Nazareth and said: *The Spirit of the Lord is upon me, because he hath anointed me to preach.*

You may say, "Yes, but that was Jesus. Of course, He was anointed of God to preach. I'm not Jesus; I'm not called and anointed by God."

Oh, yes, you are! In one of John's letters to the Church, he wrote: *But the anointing which ye have received of him abideth in you* (1 John 2:27).

The same anointing that was on Jesus is on you if you are a believer, according to the Word of God. It's in you—*it* abideth in you. Praise God! Isaiah 10:27 tells us that it is the anointing that destroys the yoke.

You **are anointed to preach the Gospel.**

The Greater One Indwells You

Ye are of God, little children, and have overcome them: because greater is he that is in you, than he that is in the world.

1 John 4:4

Never say you are unable to go out into this world and witness for Jesus. Why aren't you able? What can Satan and his demons possibly throw up in front of you that you are not more than able to overcome? The Word of God says you have already *overcome them: because greater is he that is in you, than he that is in the world.*

You are an overcomer, because **the Greater One indwells** *you.*

You Have His Ability

You **are** able to witness. You **do** have the ability—not of yourself perhaps, but you do have the ability. You have God's ability within you. You will not be going in your own strength, but in His.

Your testimony should always be that of the Apostle Paul: *I can do all things through Christ which strengtheneth me* (Phil. 4:13).

Can you see, then, what kind of effect this knowledge will have upon you if you are preparing to be an effective ambassador and representative of Jesus?

You start out by confessing what the Word of God has to say about you. Try it:

My God has not given me the spirit of fear; but of power, and of love, and of a sound mind. I have not received the spirit of a coward.

God has given me boldness. I am the righteousness of God, and, thank God, the righteous are as bold as a lion.

I have received God's anointing, and it abides within me. He has anointed me to preach good things.

Greater is He that is in me than he that is in the world.

I can do all things through Christ Who strengthens me.

When you do this, you are realizing who you are in Christ, what you are in Christ, your authority as a believer.

It is very important that you approach witnessing with a positive attitude. **You can witness effectively.** You have the Spirit of God within you, the Spirit of boldness. You are anointed by God Himself to speak good things. The One Who indwells you is greater than the one who opposes you. You have God's own ability operating inside you. **You can witness!**

3

Realize the Integrity of God's Word

So shall my word be that goeth forth out of my mouth: it shall not return unto me void, but it shall accomplish that which I please, and it shall prosper in the thing whereto I sent it.

Isaiah 55:11

God's Word Shall Not Return Void

We have already mentioned this fact, but I would like to reemphasize it here: To become an effective witness, you must learn to place absolute confidence in the integrity of God's Word. When God says something, He means what He says. When He says He will do something, it will be done.

When we plant the seed of God's Word in the hearts of people, God has said that it will not return to Him void, but that it will accomplish His purpose in that person's life.

It is not always our job to reap results, at least not immediate and visible results. It **is** our job, however, to plant the Word. We are to sow the Word of God.

He has promised that when we do, it will not return to Him void.

God Will Hasten His Word to Perform It

I will hasten my word to perform it.
Jeremiah 1:12

It should encourage you in your witnessing to know that not only will God's Word not return to Him void, but He will hasten to perform it.

Don't be overly concerned if some people don't respond instantly to your witness.

That's not always the most important thing at the moment. You have planted the seed, you have shared the Word. Just remember, God has promised that not only will it not return void, but He Himself will hasten to perform His Word in that person's life.

In other words, I am saying that if you will go forth and plant the Word, God will see to it that it is performed. You are not to worry about the results. You are to rely on the integrity of God's Word. Do your part, then rest assured that God will do His.

God's Word—A Discerner of the Thoughts and Intents of the Heart

For the word of God is quick, and powerful,
and sharper than any twoedged sword, piercing

> *even to the dividing asunder of soul and spirit,*
> *and of the joints and marrow, and is a discerner of*
> *the thoughts and intents of the heart.*
>   *Hebrews 4:12*

This fact is very important for us to realize. Many times people are moved by what they see. If they are sharing the word of reconciliation with a person, it may seem, from all outward appearances, that the person is totally uninterested in what is being said to him.

In a situation like that, we need to realize that we are not dealing with people's minds, but with their spirits.

Many times it is a little difficult for people to understand spiritual things because they are so carnally minded. The Word of God is not mentally discerned; it is spiritually discerned. (1 Cor. 2:14.) Because of this, we must always remember that we are not dealing with people's minds. It is not a person's mind which gets recreated. When we witness, we are dealing with the spirit of a man, planting the Word in his heart.

Regardless of a person's outward reaction—how he looks or what he says—I am always confident that the Word I have shared has been planted in his heart, that it has gone directly to the place that is the proper environment for God's Word—the heart.

When that person leaves me, either he will have prayed with me, or he will know how to pray—I'll see to that. You should make note of that statement: **If a person to whom I share the Lord Jesus Christ does not pray with me right then, I will see to it that before he leaves me, he knows how to pray. Then when the time comes that he is ready to accept Christ, he will know how to do so.**

I realize that there are times when people just keep right on walking when you start your introduction or approach. You may not get to share with them everything you had intended. In that case, believe that the Word you did get to share (even if it was only the name of Jesus) has been planted, that somebody else will come and water it, and that God will get the increase. That makes you a winner with everybody.

If you have the opportunity to share with someone, do your very best to see that they either pray with you right then, or know how to pray before they leave your presence. If they don't pray with you, don't be discouraged. Don't be dejected or oppressed. Rejoice because you had the opportunity to share the Word, and that Word will enter his heart and produce results. It will not return void!

There are many people who will look at you while you are sharing with them and act as though they couldn't care less about what you're saying.

They may look at you as though they're thinking, *I don't want to hear this,* but you never know what's happening in that person's heart, unless you know the integrity of God's Word.

Lots of people have just looked at me like they could hardly wait for me to leave, but I knew what was going on inside them. Do you know how I knew? Because I remember what was going on inside me when people would talk to me about Jesus. I would give them that rebellious look, like I wasn't interested in what they were saying and didn't want to hear it. But you know what? They couldn't tell what was really going on inside me.

Before Carolyn and I were married, I would come home from college on weekends to see her, and she was always telling me about the Lord. She was trying her best to get me "turned on to Jesus."

I wouldn't dare let her know that it bothered me, that what she was saying was getting to me. When I would spend a weekend at home, listening to her talk, going with her to all those youth rallies, I would act as though I could hardly wait to get away from her. I wouldn't dare let her know what was really happening to me: I couldn't stop thinking about the things she had told me about Jesus.

In the fourth chapter of Mark, Jesus told a parable about a sower who went forth to sow seed. (vv. 3-8.) He said that some seed fell to the ground on the path and was eaten up by the birds. Some fell on stony ground where there wasn't much earth; it sprang up, but soon died for lack of soil. Some fell among thorns which later choked out the young plants which sprouted up. Finally, some fell on good ground, grew up, and produced a bountiful harvest.

Later Jesus explained the parable to His disciples. (vv. 11-23.) He said that the seed represented the Word and the different types of soil represented the hearts of those who heard the Word preached.

If you will read that parable carefully, you will notice that regardless of the kind of ground in which it was sown, the Word did what it was supposed to do: It reached the heart.

Now some of the hearts in which it was sown allowed the Word to be dug up. Some allowed it to be choked out. But you will notice that in every case, when the Word was shared—regardless of whether they had no root in themselves, or whether it was stony ground, or thorny ground, or good ground—the Word did what it was designed to do: It reached the ground.

Once the Word is released from a man's mouth, it will enter the heart, as surely as sown seed will fall to the earth. That's part of the miraculous ability of the Word. It will always go to the heart, because that's the proper environment for God's Word.

Regardless of the way people may react, I approach witnessing with a positive attitude, based on God's Word. I always believe that the seed I sow (the Word I share) will lodge in the heart of the one to whom I speak.

If that person walks away from me as though he didn't care, I'm not going to be the one to dig up the seed by saying, "Well, there's one who wouldn't listen to me. There goes one who doesn't care." As far as I'm concerned, I've done my part.

When a person walks away from me like that, I just say, "Father, I've done my job. I've planted the seed. You said that Your Word wouldn't return void, but will accomplish that which You please. I know it's pleasing to You that all men come to the knowledge of the truth, because You have said so. You also said, 'How can they believe, except they hear?' I've preached and they've heard. Now I believe that they'll receive."

God's Word Gives Light

The only reason a person rebels against God is because his understanding has been blinded by Satan. But the Word gives light and removes blindness.

Psalm 119:130 says: *The entrance of thy words giveth light; it giveth understanding unto the simple.*

Paul tells us in the fourth chapter of 2 Corinthians: *But if our gospel be hid, it is hid to them that are lost . . .* (v. 3).

How do you hide the Gospel? By not sharing it!

. . . In whom the god of this world hath blinded the minds of them which believe not (v. 4).

The only reason a sinner doesn't believe is because his mind has been blinded. His understanding has been darkened. But when you give the Word, the Bible says the entrance of it gives light and understanding to the simple. God is saying, in reality, that the reason any person doesn't believe is because he is simpleminded. His understanding has been blinded.

I'm sure you know as well as I that the only reason you didn't accept Jesus any sooner than you did is because you didn't have a good understanding of the Gospel. Your mind, your understanding, was blinded. But then you heard the truth. What happened? Do you remember what you said? "I see it. It has finally dawned on me." That's what I said too. And "dawn" is the entrance of light, isn't it?

That's why the Bible says the entrance of God's Word gives light. It's possible to hear the Gospel—and hear it, and hear it, and hear it—then suddenly the light is turned on. Suddenly, you see it. Everything you had heard all that time, everything you had stored up inside, became very clear. You listened to the Gospel over and over, and the moment you heard some particular truth, you recalled all that was stored up inside and you said, "Oh, so that's what that means! Now I understand it. I see it now. That's simple."

This is exactly what happens to the sinner when he finally "sees" the truth of the Gospel. He becomes "enlightened," doesn't he? You see, Satan has blinded the mind of the sinner.

Stop and think about it for a moment. If the sinner knew Satan—if he could see him just the way he really is—and if he knew God—if he could see Him just the way He really is—there is not the slightest doubt which of them he would choose. The sinner would choose God—immediately! Then why hasn't he already done so? Very simple. The only reason the sinner has not already chosen God is because his mind has been blinded by Satan.

Nobody in his right mind would ever deliberately choose Satan over God, any more than he would consciously choose to go to hell rather than to heaven. So there must be something wrong with the mind of a person who doesn't choose God. That's right, there certainly is—his mind is blinded.

In some cases, the sinner's mind is so blinded that he doesn't even believe there is a Devil or a hell. In some other cases, the sinner believes there is a Devil, but he doesn't know the truth about him. He may believe there is a God, but he doesn't know the truth about God. In other words, the eyes of his understanding have been blinded or darkened to the truth about them.

But the entrance of God's Word gives light and brings understanding to the simple. In order for the sinner to be born again, the "blinders" must be removed from him. How do you remove the blinders? By the Word. You share God's Word, and it will cause light to come. When that light enters a sinner's heart, he will see Jesus for Who He is and gladly choose Him.

The god of this world—Satan—has blinded the mind of the sinner; but, thank God, the Word has the ability to give understanding to the blinded mind. We need to have a revelation of the integrity and the power of God's Word. That will give us the courage, the boldness, and the confidence we need to share the Good News with people who need to hear it.

I have these things in my mind constantly. I don't know how it affects you, but when I get ready to share Jesus with somebody—a total stranger, if that's the case—these things go off inside me. Immediately I begin to think:

I have received power because the Holy Ghost has come upon me and I am an effective witness. Thank God, I can guarantee, vouche for, and prove what I

have seen and heard and know, because God works in me confirming His Word with signs following.

I don't have the spirit of fear. I'm not a coward. I can do all things through Christ Who strengthens me. Greater is He that's in me than he that's in the world. I have boldness because I'm the righteousness of God, and the righteous are bold as a lion.

Thank God, it's the Word that's going to get this person born again. The entrance of the Word is going to give light and the blinders are going to be removed from his understanding.

This works like a checklist inside me. I approach it with a very positive attitude, expecting results. I don't enjoy wasting time on things that are nonproductive. If all I can expect when I make myself available to witness is no results, then I'm going to do something else—something more productive.

You will always get exactly what you believe for. Jesus said, *According to your faith be it unto you* (Matt. 9:29).

Let me show you what I mean. Several years ago as I was ministering in a church in Oklahoma City, Kenneth Copeland called my home in Shreveport and told my wife to have me meet him in Jacksonville Beach, Florida. When I finished my meeting there in

Oklahoma City, we drove to Jacksonville Beach to meet Brother Copeland. He was conducting a series of meetings there in a place called the Beaches Auditorium.

There were lots of kids out on the beach who were involved in the drug culture. Brother Copeland wanted me to set up some witnessing seminars in his crusade. So every afternoon we met together between his morning and evening meetings. After each session, we would go out on the beach so the people could put into practice what they were learning about witnessing.

During that series of meetings, 150 people responded to Brother Copeland's invitation to accept the Lord Jesus Christ as their personal Savior. The number of people we won out on the beach matched that number. We led as many people to the Lord on a one-to-one basis as Brother Copeland did by preaching in the auditorium.

But the most amazing thing was that most of the people who were doing the witnessing were people who had just been born again themselves.

I will never forget one experience I had during that time. One day when we went out to witness, I had just gotten on the beach when several young girls came up to me and asked for some money. So I started sharing the Word with them. As I was speaking, they began to look at one another; and then, one by one, they began to cry. I had been on the beach only a few minutes when all six of those young girls got born again. Then they followed us around, leading other people to the Lord.

Another time there was a drunken sailor who was sitting on a bench. I sat down next to him and tapped him on the shoulder. When he turned and looked at me, I said, "Sir, I'd like to share something with you that has changed my whole life."

"What is it?"

"Well, I want to tell you about Jesus."

"I don't want to hear it."

"Well, I've just got to tell you this. It's changed my whole life and I want Him to do something for you."

When he got up to walk away, I said, "Where are you going?"

"I don't want to hear it."

"Well," I said, "do you mind if I walk with you?"

"Okay," he said, "but don't tell me about Jesus." So I told him about Paul—about Paul's conversion.

When he turned and started walking the other way, I asked, "Do you mind if I walk with you?"

"No, I don't mind," he said. "Just don't tell me about Jesus or Paul." So I told him about Peter!

As I walked up and down that beach with him, he would say, "I don't want to hear it." Then he would turn and walk in the other direction, so I would just follow him. Finally we stopped in front of a snack bar. He looked at me and said, "Why are you following me? Why don't you leave me alone?"

"Sir, I can't. When I saw you sitting on that bench, the Spirit of God prompted me to come and share with you. God wants to do something for you. He wants to do something in your life right now. You need Jesus in a desperate way."

He started crying. I shared the Lord with him, told him how to get born again, and asked him if there was any reason why he couldn't accept Jesus right then.

He said, "No, there isn't."

I prayed with him, and he accepted Jesus as Lord of his life. Then he told me, "I'm so glad you wouldn't let me alone. I'm glad you kept following me. I just got a dishonorable discharge from the Navy. I've been in for over twenty years and was just about to retire. Then I did something I knew I shouldn't have done and spent time in jail for it. So I got a dishonorable discharge. My family doesn't know about it. I've been sitting here on this bench for a week. They think I'm still in San Diego."

Then he looked at me with a smile and said, "I'm so glad you wouldn't leave me alone. I can face them now and know that everything will be all right."

Praise God! If that doesn't straighten out your day, nothing will!

You have that ability, and God will work with you, confirming the Word with signs following. When you know without a doubt who you are in Christ and you know the integrity of the Word, then you won't be afraid. When you know that God has not given you the spirit of a coward, timidity will leave you. Jesus said, *Ye shall receive power, after that the Holy Ghost is come upon you: and ye shall be witnesses unto me.* **Realize who you are in Christ. Realize that God has enabled you and empowered you to do it.**

Another thing you need to realize is that the world is waiting for you. Your neighbor is waiting. The guy at the grocery store is waiting. The fellow down at the service station is waiting. They are waiting—for you!

I've had more fun leading service station attendants and waitresses to the Lord. It's fun!

One day I was in Birmingham, Alabama. When I got off the airplane, a taxi driver took me to the hotel. Before I got to the hotel, I had led the taxi driver to the Lord. When I got to the hotel, I led the maid to the Lord too. It's not hard to win souls!

We are effective witnesses in the sight of God because He has empowered us to be so. What we need to do is start seeing ourselves the way God sees us.

You can be an effective witness for Jesus Christ. Would you like to do that? If so, then pray this prayer of commitment right now. Say this out loud:

In the name of Jesus, I have received power—miracle-working ability—for I have received the Holy Ghost. I am bold as the lion of Judah. I am the righteousness of God, and the righteous are bold as a lion.

God has not given me a spirit of fear, but of power, and of love, and of a sound mind. I am not a coward. In the name of Jesus, I have boldness. Through Him, by Him, and with Him I can do all things for the Greater One dwells within me. Greater is He that is in me than he that is in the world.

Heavenly Father, I am Your ambassador. If You are looking for someone to send, here am I—send me. I'll go. I'm Your ambassador. I'm Your representative. I expect You to work with me confirming the Word with signs following, for I'm bold as a lion.

The world awaits me. The lost await me. In the name of Jesus, I am wise because I win souls for the Kingdom of God.

Thank You, Lord, for making me an effective witness for You. Praise the Lord! Amen.

4
Before You Go . . .

Now that you have made the commitment to witness actively, to share Jesus effectively with others, let me now give you some suggestions (from my own experiences) which I believe will greatly increase the effectiveness of your ministry.

The first suggestion I would make to anyone who is about to go out witnessing is to bind the Devil and loose the ministering angels. Both are scriptural, and both are vitally important for effective witnessing.

Bind the Strong Man

In Matthew 12:29 Jesus asked the Pharisees, *How can one enter a strong man's house, and spoil his goods, except he first bind the strong man? and then he will spoil his house.* Another translation puts it this way: "If you're going to spoil the strong man's house, you must first bind him."

In our case, the strong man would be Satan. When you go out into the world to win souls, it is Satan's "house" you are entering, his "territory," and he will not allow you to come in and "spoil his house" without putting up some opposition.

That's why I always suggest that you bind the Devil so he can't interfere. Your first question, then, would be: "When do we do that? After we get out there?" No. I suggest that you bind the strong man before you ever go. If you take care of Satan before you go, you won't have to put up with him when you get out there.

I remember the first time the Spirit of God taught me this lesson. As I took groups of people out with me to witness, to share Jesus, many of them would come back and say, "You know, I'm getting tired of people arguing with me. I'm tired of them coming up with some religious doctrine to argue about when I'm trying to share Jesus with them."

I remember one time when I was sharing Jesus with an elderly man in a shopping center. Only five or six words had come out of my mouth when he interrupted me.

"What about evolution?" he asked.

"Well, what about it?"

He answered, "Well, I believe . . ." Then he went on and on, expounding to me what he believed.

I have since learned to keep control of the conversation; otherwise, people will lead you off on all kinds of tangents, into religious discussions and debates, and you'll never get back to the point you wanted to make.

It is very important to remember: **Keep control of the conversation.** If you don't, you may end up spending an hour and a half listening to someone tell about all kinds of things. Then you end up discouraged because you never got to share the Good News with him.

When I deal with a person who wants to lead the conversation off into a religious discussion or debate, I just very politely say, "Listen, let me share this with you first. Then I'll be happy to discuss those things with you. Okay? I've got something I want to share with you that I believe is very important." You can do that very nicely without offending the person or hurting his feelings.

What you want to do is get the Word out. Then you can talk about doctrines afterwards, if necessary. I've found that if I can control the conversation and just keep putting the Word out, most of the time we never get to those silly questions. We never get around to those religious discussions. Somehow when the Word goes out, those old religious speculations don't mean anything anymore.

Let me give you an example of what I'm talking about when I say we need to bind Satan before we go so he can't interfere.

One time while I was in Oklahoma City, a group was sharing Jesus in a shopping center called

Shepherd Mall. Quite often we would take a group of young people there to witness. One night we left the church, went to the mall, and spread out to meet and talk with people in different parts of the mall.

In a little while one girl came back to me and said, "Brother Savelle, do you see that guy sitting over there by himself?"

"Yes."

"Well, I'm having a lot of problems with him. All he wants to do is argue with me. How do you handle that?"

I gave her some instructions and she went back. In a few minutes, here she came again.

"Brother Savelle, he's still arguing."

"Why don't you let somebody else share with him for a little while. Let the other person do the talking while you just pray."

She found someone to go with her to talk to this young man, but in a little while they both came back with the same story. "This guy's something else! All he wants to do is argue. We can't get a word in edgewise! What'll we do?"

By this time others were coming back, saying, "I've never seen so many religious people who want to talk about doctrines. What should we do?"

At that very moment I was trying to share with a Jehovah's Witness. I want you to know, friend, that when you approach a Jehovah's Witness, you had better know your business, because they are indoctrinated with their doctrines!

There I was sharing with this person and finding it a little difficult to get through to him. Then here come all these kids complaining about how much trouble they were having. It seemed like we just weren't getting anywhere.

Suddenly, the Spirit of God said something to me—something very simple. I'll never forget it. It has been a tremendous help to me ever since. He said, "Son, if you would bind the Devil before you come out here, you wouldn't have to put up with this."

I thought, *Isn't that simple? Why didn't I think of that earlier?*

He said, "If all of you would join together in agreement and bind the Devil in the lives of the people you're going to be ministering to—before you ever get to them—you won't have this problem."

So we started doing that. Instead of waiting until we got out and ran into these pressures, we decided to bind the Devil before we left the church. Then we expected him to be bound when we got there. From then on, we didn't have those problems.

I remember one other rather unusual situation during that time. The kids were talking to one young man who had just come back from Vietnam. He was just passing through town, wandering aimlessly around the country, hanging around shopping malls to pass away the time. About three or four of our kids had shared with him that night, but he just argued with them and wouldn't listen to what they had to say.

The next night we left half of the people in Shepherd Mall and took the other half to a place called Penn Square Shopping Center. This young man from Vietnam had decided that since all those "Jesus freaks" (as he called us) were at Shepherd Mall, he would go over to Penn Square where he wouldn't be bothered. But when he got there, we were waiting! When somebody else approached him and shared with him, he didn't receive it too well and wanted to argue.

The next night he went back to Shepherd Mall, thinking that we were at Penn Square now. When we walked in, there he was sitting on a bench. When he saw us come in, he just shook his head like he couldn't believe it. A couple of the kids went over to him. They had such a love for that young man. They wanted him to get born again so badly that they decided they just couldn't quit talking to him, even if he didn't want to listen. They had no more success with him this time than before. In a little while they brought him to me and asked him if he would please talk to me.

He sat down, and I shared with him for at least an hour. He told me about his experiences in Vietnam. The reason he didn't believe in God was because of all the men he had seen die over there. "If God's real, then why did He let everybody get killed?" He was really serious, concerned and confused in his mind.

As we talked, I just shared with him about God and the ministry of reconciliation. I talked to him about what that meant to him personally. He listened for a while, but was still a little hesitant about it all, so I invited him to go with us. Each evening when we finished witnessing, we went to the church fellowship hall for refreshments. We brought in all the people we had led to the Lord, just to have a time of fellowship with them. We got their names and addresses for follow-up purposes and gave them our names and addresses. We wanted them to know that if they ever needed help, we were available.

At first, this fellow was hesitant about going with us; but he finally decided to go. He didn't have anything else to do. When he saw the love of Jesus among all those young people and realized that we weren't just a bunch of religious fanatics, spouting "thou shalt not's," he began to loosen up. Everybody made him feel welcome and comfortable. He recognized, after all, that there was truth in all that we had been telling him. Finally, he prayed with one of the people to receive Jesus and was born again.

From that experience we learned the importance of binding Satan before we go out. He is the strong man in this situation—the one who has blinded the minds and understanding of the lost. Jesus said that if we are going to enter the strong man's house, we must first bind him. Then we can go in and spoil his house.

Psalm 111:6 says, *He hath shewed his people the power of his works, that he may give them the heritage of the heathen.* God is telling us that He has empowered His people with His own miracle virtue to enable them to claim their inheritance of unregenerated souls. **These unregenerated souls are part of our inheritance as ambassadors for Christ.** Causing these unregenerated souls to be made new creations is part of our inheritance. God has empowered us to do that.

But always remember: Bind the Devil before you go out to spoil his house. You spoil Satan's house by taking those unregenerated souls and making them new creations.

Loose the Ministering Spirits

First, you bind the Devil, but that's not all you do before you go. There is another important step to be taken. You need to loose God's ministering spirits to work with you.

In Matthew 18:18 Jesus says:

> *Verily I say unto you, Whatsoever ye shall bind on earth shall be bound in heaven: and whatsoever ye shall loose on earth shall be loosed in heaven.*

The writer of Hebrews says about the angels of God: *Are they not all ministering spirits, sent forth to minister **for them** who shall be heirs of salvation?* (Heb. 1:14).

I want you to know that we Christians have been given charge of all the angels of God! The Bible says that they are sent forth to minister for us who are the heirs of salvation.

Before I go out to share Jesus with people, I bind Satan because he is the strong man in this case. I bind him. I render him helpless and paralyzed. He is the spirit who is controlling the lives of those people, so I render him helpless. Then I loose the ministering angels to go before me and prepare the people to receive the light of the Gospel. I bind Satan from interfering, and I loose the ministering spirits to do their work.

I expect the angels of God to go before me and prepare the people to receive the truth that I will bring. It works. I've seen it work. There have been times when I have gone to people's homes and they would say, "You know, I just knew that I was going to get born again tonight. I just knew that something was going to happen to me tonight." Why? Because I had bound the Devil and loosed the ministering spirits before I ever left home.

In John 6:44 Jesus said, *No man can come to me, except the Father which hath sent me draw him.* I want that person to be drawn to God before I ever get there. If he has already been drawn when I get there, then my job is very easy. The Devil is bound so that he can't interfere. The person is drawn; his spirit is open to receive. All I have to do is give him the Good News.

Don't misunderstand me. I am not saying that every person you deal with is going to be very easy to win, that there will be little or no effort required on your part. I am saying that if you will begin to develop a very positive attitude about this, it will become easier.

Let me give you an example to illustrate what I mean. Let's imagine that the first person you share with is absolutely the rudest person you have ever met in your life. In the natural, the first thing you would want to do is quit. That would be your natural reaction, right? Immediately the Devil would jump right into the middle of you and say, "Everybody you share with tonight is going to be the same way. You're wasting your time, you fool."

But you can't be moved by that. You can't allow yourself to become discouraged. You must remember that Satan is helpless to interfere and that the ministering spirits are at work with you.

First, you bind the Devil, then you loose the ministering spirits to draw those people and place them in a position where you can approach them. Then when you do, they are ready to receive the Word—the glorious light of the Gospel. And what will happen? The entrance of the Word gives light and understanding to the simple.

Jesus said, *The harvest truly is great, but the labourers are few: pray ye the Lord of the harvest, that he would send forth labourers into his harvest* (Luke 10:2). We are those laborers, and the fields are awaiting us!

Bind the Devil, loose the angels, and go. Then when you go, expect results.

Expect Results

And he said unto them, Go ye into all the world, and preach the gospel to every creature. He that believeth and is baptized shall be saved; but he that believeth not shall be damned.

And these signs shall follow them that believe; In my name shall they cast out devils; they shall speak with new tongues; they shall take up serpents; and if they drink any deadly thing, it shall not hurt them; they shall lay hands on the sick, and they shall recover.

So then after the Lord had spoken unto them, he was received up into heaven, and sat on the right hand of God.

And they went forth, and preached every where, the Lord working with them, and confirming the word with signs following.
Mark 16:15-20

This is the reason you can expect results: You are going forth as an ambassador for Jesus, and the Lord will work with you.

Matthew said it this way: *And, lo, I am with you alway, even unto the end of the world* (Matt. 28:20).

The Lord worked with them. Doing what? Confirming. . . . *confirming the word with signs following.*

I expect results because I know that God is faithful. I don't go out on my merits; I go on His merit. He is faithful Who has promised. (Heb. 10:23.) Mark said of the disciples that the Lord worked with them, confirming the Word with signs following. So when I go, I expect results. I expect the Father God to work with me and to confirm His Word with signs following.

In the second chapter of Acts, we read how Peter stood up on the day of Pentecost and preached the Word to the Jews who had gathered in Jerusalem. Let's read about it. Let's see if God confirmed His Word for Peter and if Peter got any kind of results.

Now when they heard this (Peter's testimony), *they were pricked in their heart, and said unto Peter and to the rest of the apostles, Men and brethren, what shall we do?*

Then Peter said unto them, Repent, and be baptized every one of you in the name of Jesus Christ for the remission of sins, and ye shall receive the gift of the Holy Ghost. For the promise is unto you, and to your children, and to all that are afar off, even as many as the Lord our God shall call.

And with many other words did he testify and exhort, saying, Save yourselves from this untoward generation.

Then they that **gladly** *received his word were baptized: and the same day there were added unto them about three thousand souls.*

Acts 2:37-41

In Acts 4:1-4 we read:

And as they (Peter and John) *spake unto the people, the priests, and the captain of the temple, and the Sadducees, came upon them, being grieved that they taught the people, and preached through Jesus the resurrection from the dead.*

And they laid hands on them, and put them in hold unto the next day: for it was now eventide.

Howbeit **many of them which heard the word believed;** *and the number of the men was about five thousand.*

113

Notice this says, . . . *them which heard the word believed.* Do you remember Romans 10:14,15? It says, *How shall they believe in him of whom they have not heard? and how shall they hear without a preacher? and how shall they preach, except they be sent?*

How can they believe unless they hear the Word? When you go, you are to speak the Word. Then when you speak the Word, you should expect results.

Go in Pairs

Now this is just a suggestion, but I have a good reason for making it. In Luke 10:1 we read that when Jesus appointed the seventy to go and preach the Gospel, *he sent them two and two.*

Now I'm not saying that you cannot or should not go on your own and witness on a one-to-one basis. I'm not saying that at all. You can witness to people individually and personally everywhere you go.

My suggestion is that in a group soulwinning endeavor, such as those organized by a church, you should go out in pairs. The reason I suggest this is so that while one is sharing, the other can pray. You will find this to be very beneficial, especially in the difficult situations you sometimes encounter such as when a person just wants to argue. The Bible says that one can chase a thousand, and two can put ten thousand to flight. (Deut. 32:30.) If you have one doing the talking and another doing the praying, then you have strength.

Now, one other point . . . When you approach someone, be sure that only one person does the talking. If you are sharing, but sense in your spirit that you aren't getting anywhere, stop right at that moment and say to your partner, "Listen, why don't you share with him your testimony?" Then let your partner talk.

While your partner is talking, you should pray. By doing this, you aren't "ganging up" on the person. You are ganging up on the Devil! You will find that it strengthens you as you share to know someone is praying for you.

The person praying should pray like this:

1. **Pray for the one who is sharing.** Your prayer should be specific and to the point. You should pray two things: that the Spirit of God will give that person utterance that he may open his mouth boldly to make known the mystery of the Gospel; and that the Word of God will have free course in him, that it will flow freely, and that the person to whom he is speaking will not be able to resist the wisdom and the spirit by which he speaks. (Eph. 6:19; Acts 6:10.)

2. **Pray for the person with whom you are sharing.** Again, be specific in your praying. Pray these two things: that he have ears to hear—to hear the Word and to hear the wisdom of God flowing through the mouth of the one who is sharing; and that the eyes of his understanding be enlightened so that he knows the hope of God's calling and the riches of the glory of His inheritance. (Matt. 11:15; Eph. 1:18.)

You are thus praying that this person might hear the Gospel and receive it in his spirit, and that the eyes of his spirit might be opened so that he can understand what God has done for him in Christ Jesus.

When one person is speaking forth wisdom which cannot be resisted, and the other is praying and keeping Satan in his place, then there is strength in your witnessing. That knowledge gives confidence to the one who is sharing and breaks down the walls of indifference and resistance so that the Word can reach that person's heart and do its work.

5

Sample Approach

Now I would like to give you a sample approach in sharing Jesus. This is not necessarily meant to be a model for you to imitate word for word. It is intended rather as an example of the way you might approach and share Jesus with a person you have never met.

How do you approach a total stranger? Do you just "accidentally" bump into him and say, "Oh, excuse me, I'd like to share something with you"? I suppose you could, but that's not exactly what I would recommend.

So how do you start? The first thing you need to consider is: Who do you approach? The answer is fairly simple. Most of the time it's best to begin with someone who is not in a hurry and who obviously has nothing else to do but listen to you. Don't try to out talk somebody who is walking as fast as he can to catch a bus. That won't work!

If the person you approach isn't in a hurry, both of you will be more at ease. Then that person is free to give you his full attention.

Once you have chosen the person, how do you initiate the conversation? How do you get into what you want to share?

In my own personal approach, I usually say something like, "Hello, I'd like to share something with you that's changed my whole life." Or I might just walk up and introduce myself: "Hello, I'm Jerry Savelle, and I'd like to share something with you that has changed my whole life."

As you will see on this sample approach, I sometimes say, "Hello, my name is Jerry Savelle. I want to ask you something. Have you heard the Good News?" That's a good way to get a person's attention, isn't it? After all, everybody (especially these days) is interested in hearing some good news for a change.

Now this person doesn't know anything about what I want to say. It might be anything. It may be that the federal government is not going to make us pay income tax anymore. (That would be good news!) He has no earthly idea of what I'm going to talk to him about at this point, but he is interested to hear it—no matter what it is. If it's good news, he *wants* to hear it. And that's the important thing. First of all, I want to get his attention.

I don't go up to him and say, "Hey, you—do you believe in God? Do you go to church? Are you a sinner?" I don't want to say anything that will put him on the defensive. I surely don't want to approach with: "You're going to hell if you don't listen to me!"

I want to say something that will get his attention. How can he believe except he hear?

I don't want to turn him off with my approach, and I don't want to get into a religious discussion or debate. You will find that most people you share with, especially in the "Bible belt," have been to church at least once in their lives. Most of them think that because they have been that one time, all is well. Those that have been to church a few times think they know a little something about religion. If you go up to them and say, "I'd like to talk to you about God," they will likely say, "Oh, I go to church." But you don't want to hear that right then. You want to get their attention.

My initial approach is: "I'd like to share something with you that has changed my whole life." At this point I haven't introduced anything, but I have that person's attention. He will usually give me enough time to introduce to him what changed my life. For the most part, everybody out there is looking for something that will change their lives. Once I have his attention, then I can lead him into the Good News and share Jesus with him.

Now let's look at an example of how your conversation might go:

"Say, have you heard the Good News? Did you know that Jesus is alive, and that He wants to make

Himself real to you right now? Jesus said, *He that loveth me shall be loved of my Father, and I will love him, and will manifest myself* (or make Myself real) *to him.* Jesus wants to make Himself real to you right now.

"God loved you so very much that even while you were a sinner, Christ died for you. But, listen, that's not where it stops. The Bible also says that God made Jesus Christ, Who knew no sin, to be sin for you, so that you might be made the righteousness of God. Do you know what "righteousness" means? Well, let me tell you. Righteousness just simply means right standing with God. Did you know that you have right standing with God, that God has already forgiven you, that He is not holding anything against you?

"The Bible says that it was God personally present in Christ, reconciling and restoring the world to favor with Himself—not counting up and holding men's sins against them, but canceling them. Did you know that God has already forgiven you of your sins? Now, tell me, isn't that good news?

"Now listen to this. The Bible says that we, being justified by faith, have peace with God through our Lord Jesus Christ. Did you know that because of what God has already done through His Son Jesus Christ at Calvary, He has already forgiven you and would like to manifest Himself to you right now?

"Do you know how He does that? The Bible says when you confess with your mouth that Jesus is Lord and believe in your heart that God has raised Him from the dead, then you will be saved. Jesus has promised that He would then come and live in you and make Himself real to you. Isn't that great?

"Not too long ago I was unhappy and miserable. But then somebody shared this good news with me and I accepted Jesus as Lord of my life that day. I want you to know that since that day, I have lived the high life. Jesus delivered me and transformed my whole life, all because I believed that He is the Son of God and that God has raised Him from the dead.

"Let me ask you something. Is there any reason why you can't make Jesus the Lord of your life right now? I'd like to pray with you. Would you let me pray with you?"

Now, that isn't hard, is it?

Then you lead that person in a simple confession of the lordship of Jesus Christ—not a confession of sins. The sinner doesn't confess sins to get born again; he confesses the lordship of Jesus Christ.

Here is an example of the kind of simple prayer I lead people in:

O God in heaven, I accept Your love and Your forgiveness for my life right now. I believe in my heart and I confess with my mouth that Jesus Christ is the Son of God, and that You have raised Him from the dead. I make Him the Lord of my life now.

I renounce my past life with sin and Satan, and I thank You for receiving me as Your child.

From this moment forward, my life belongs to Jesus, and Him only I shall serve. Thank You for making Yourself real to me right now. Amen.''

When having the person pray with you, encourage him to repeat the prayer so that he can hear himself declaring that Jesus is Lord.

6
Follow-Up

Once the person has prayed this prayer and made Jesus the Lord of his life, then you want him to know that he is a new creation. You want him to understand what has happened to him and who he is in Christ. Don't just let him go on his way right then. He needs some follow-up to help him in his new Christian walk and to get him involved in a good church where he can learn and develop.

The first thing I do is get his name, address, and telephone number. Then I offer him mine because he will need a friend. He is just a babe in Christ and will need counseling and support until he reaches some maturity.

If he is from your own area, you can help provide that support. If he doesn't live near you, then do your best to guide him to a church or assembly where you know he will get the instruction he needs.

When I lead a person to the Lord, even in my own city of Fort Worth, I don't insist that he become a member of my church. I really don't care where he goes to church, as long as it is a solid Word church. If he asks what church I recommend, I don't hesitate to tell him. But my purpose is not to get more people into my church. My purpose is to get him born again.

If he doesn't know a good place to worship, I don't say that just any place will do. Just any place will not do! I want him in a place where he's going to be fed the Word and where he will have an opportunity to grow properly.

Guide (**don't** try to pressure or force) him to a good Word church where he will grow *unto the measure of the stature of the fulness of Christ* (Eph. 4:13).

Finally, if you sense in your spirit that he is in a position right then to receive, don't hesitate to share more with him. Sit down and share the Word with him concerning being filled with the Holy Spirit.

I believe with all my heart that if you will take these instructions and suggestions and apply them to your own witnessing, you too will see that you can share Jesus effectively.

God bless you as you go into all the world and give the Gospel of Jesus Christ to every creature!

Jerry Savelle is a noted author, evangelist, and Bible teacher who travels extensively throughout the United States. Jerry teaches the uncompromising Word of God with a power and authority that is exciting, but with a love that delivers the message directly to the heart. His down-to-earth approach and dynamic illustrations clearly present the absolute authority of God's Word.

At the age of twelve as Jerry was watching the healing ministry of Oral Roberts on television, God spoke to his heart and called him into the ministry. Several years later, on February 11, 1969, Jerry made Jesus Christ the Lord of his life.

Since that time, he has been moving in the light of God's calling on his life. Prior to entering his own ministry, Jerry was an associate minister with Kenneth Copeland Evangelistic Association.

The scope of Jerry Savelle Ministries is far reaching as Jerry travels throughout the United States, Canada, Africa, Australia and other parts of the world.

The anointing of God upon Jerry's life is powerful, and people are set free as the Word goes forth unhindered.

For a complete list of tapes and books by Jerry Savelle, write:

Jerry Savelle Ministries
P.O. Box 2228
Fort Worth, TX 76113

Books by Jerry Savelle

The Nature of Faith

You Can Have Abundant Life

Energizing Your Faith

Man's Crown of Glory

Living In Divine Prosperity

If Satan Can't Steal Your Joy . . .

Victory & Success Are Yours!

Giving: The Essence of Living

Sharing Jesus Effectively

The Spirit of Might

A Right Mental Attitude

Sowing in Famine

Giving Birth to a Miracle

The Established Heart

Fruits of Righteousness

Godly Wisdom for Prosperity

God's Provision for Healing

Available at your local bookstore.

Harrison House

P. O. Box 35035 • Tulsa, OK 74153